To Bill
Regards from
Carroll

A
GREAT
ADVENTURE

THIRTY YEARS IN
DIPLOMATIC SERVICE

BY
CARROLL RUSSELL SHERER

Printed in the United States of America
by The Stinehour Press, Lunenburg, VT

First Edition 2007

ISBN 978-0-615-16559-2

Designed by Mary Kornblum, CMYK Design Inc.
Produced by Della R. Mancuso, Mancuso Associates Inc.

www.agreatadventure.com

THIS BOOK IS DEDICATED TO ALBERT W. SHERER, JR.
AND FRANCIS E. MELOY, JR.
TWO REMARKABLE PUBLIC SERVANTS WHO
WERE FRIENDS TO THE END.

Contents

Foreword

T HERE WAS NO TIME TO GROW UP in those days. We were like bulls in the holding pen waiting to get into the fight. We raced in without asking a lot of questions and without answering a lot of questions, including those coming from our parents. That was the way it started for us, the "Greatest Generation." We had no doubts about the outcome. We were sure of ourselves in a way we have never been since, so from that point of view, it was a comfortable time. It was no surprise that we had to work, every one of us, even the 4F's and the Conscientious Objectors. After the war was over and it had turned out the expected way, a lot of us kept on going, fighting for our entrenched values.

Now I am old. I can feel my brain cells dying, driblets every day. I realize that my fifty-seven-year-old son is really not growing taller, the way it seems. So the time has come to record whatever I remember about how our dreams played out for better and for worse.

I think all this now while I am sitting on the cement floor in the basement of the apartment house where I have lived in Chicago, sorting through a trunk of fabric remnants. I am preparing to move, and this job is part of the onerous task of separating the "take" from the "dump." But I am beginning to enjoy it. Here is the covering that was on the love seat in the living room in Morocco where we spent three years. I can see the whole room now, and right next to it in the trunk is a piece of a blouse I had made in Budapest. I had an excellent dressmaker there named Ilonka. I see her, too, as clearly as though she was sitting next to me here on the cold floor. Those were bad old days in Eastern Europe but the blouse was pretty, flashy red silk with rhinestone buttons I bought in Paris. Ilonka hadn't had materials like that to work with for a long time.

My husband, Albert, called Bud by his friends, graduated from Yale in 1938 majoring in International Relations. He wanted to go into the Foreign Service immediately but his father advised against it. The reasoning was that his son should have a second string to his bow. Perhaps he couldn't afford the life he was choosing. So Albert Jr. went to law school at Harvard, where one of his best boyhood pals was in the same class. Albert always told me how little satisfaction he derived from law school, but a couple of times years later that credential came in very handy. What he spent a lot of time doing (instead of studying the law like Potter Stewart who was number one in the class) was learning how to fly, that is to fly an airplane. Even though he got a degree, he claimed not to have excelled in law school and looking back, the reasons are obvious.

The immediate future for the United States was dim. The Second World War was on the horizon, but the role of the United States was not yet clearly in view. The next summer, however, in 1941 just as he was graduating, it became apparent to those who studied carefully, that the war was inevitable for us and coming soon. Single men who had completed their formal education would be drafted right away. Bud's passion for flying was calling, so he applied to the Army Air Corps as a pilot but was rejected at first because his eyesight was not sharp enough.

He was so eager to be admitted before he was drafted that he claimed he stayed in a dark room for three days drinking carrot juice. (And he was the sort of man you believed no matter what he said.) After that, the Air Force accepted him gladly to be schooled as a navigator, and intensive training began. He was chosen to navigate the plane taking General Arnold to the Casablanca Conference where the general was to accompany President Roosevelt attending his first consultation with Churchill and Stalin. He told me that the effort to keep the mission secret was so intense that neither he nor the pilot knew where they would end up. They simply followed the headings provided them before takeoff. During the conference he stayed out at the U.S. military base reading the news about what was going on in a meeting that altered the course of world history. But after all, he was only the chauffeur.

It was shortly after this that I met him. Our parents were long-time friends in Chicago and trying not to reveal how fervently they hoped we would be interested in each other. A few years later we both knew that it was a mutual "coup de foudre". I had a hard time revealing my end of it at first because I was too afraid that I would lose him; he would surely find someone more appealing and drift off. It was due to a seven-year difference in our ages that we had not traveled in the same circles before that. I was still a college student, second year, studying anthropology at the University of Chicago, and working hard to graduate the next year. We could do that then because Robert Hutchins, a famous and imaginative educator was experimenting in education in a way that fitted my purposes fine. I was permitted to take any examinations I wished, take extra courses, go to summer school, any plan I invented that would meet requirements to achieve my goal of graduating in three years.

I was nineteen years old then and, like everyone else in my generation, searching for an occupation that would contribute to the war effort. I joined the Cadet Nursing Corps, a federal program designed to train girls in a hurry to replace the registered nurses who had joined the armed forces. Uncle Sam paid for tuition, uniforms, books, food and housing. But my father wanted to pay the tuition himself because he secretly hoped I would find something else to do before completing the two-and-a-half year course. He explained that it was not correct to accept government funds from a program I might not finish. Although I had every intention of finishing, I didn't argue.

As I look back, it turned out to be the most valuable formal education I had, even though I didn't realize it then. The discipline I experienced was tough. Two of the head teachers must have been jealous of my previous education, which caused them to be severe with me. I decided soon that I would have to prove myself by doing superior work, so I memorized every lesson and could spout it back verbatim. That was a little protection, and of course I tried to be super-affable, which worked with everyone but my roommate named Miss Smith. She took great exception to the fact that I had a silver fox scarf, an old thing my mother had passed down to me, which I should have left at home, but I couldn't have guessed that it could be the source of trouble. I don't remember ever wearing it. My life consisted of studying and working and trying to find enough time to sleep. That's all I remember about Miss Smith, although she taught me a lot about people, which I hope I have not forgotten.

We students were housed at first in the old Stevens Hotel (now the Hilton), which had previously been commandeered by the Army and used as barracks. By the time the Cadet Nurses got there, it had become the storage location for the furniture from the French ocean liner *Normandy*, which had been turned into a troop transport ship. There were huge red upholstered chairs piled high in the lobby and fancy tables set on end. I used to wonder, "What have you seen, red chairs? My parents took a trip on the *Normandy*. Did one of them sit on you? And what sort of life will you have after this is all over?" Walking through the red chairs at night to get to the elevator was extremely spooky because the lights were turned down to a bare minimum to save energy.

Now back to my trunk. Here's a piece of the sofa fabric I used later in our house in Washington. I still have that wonderful Hungarian sofa in my life, and it is still painful to think how I happened to acquire it from a family being deported by the Communist government to the Hortobagy, a semi-desert area, with only what they could carry. That was because they did not qualify as "trustworthy people". They were unfortunate in having some sort of title, which made them expendable. The story would have made a heartrending soap opera, since it was unlikely they would ever see their grandchildren again. This was their lot because their son had married a chambermaid, which qualified his children to be classified "trustworthy people" like their mother. Try to imagine what kind of hullabaloo that wedding caused in the family! Maybe they deserved what they got, but the punishment seemed extreme to me then and it still does.

Funny, I don't find anything from the apartment in Prague where we were assigned in 1955. Our quarters had been cobbled together from rooms previously used as office space, and finally I remember I was invited to furnish it with leftovers from the Army housing authorities in Nurnberg. Survival there demanded that I hone some skills I didn't even know I had. A lot happened in that strange apartment. I will get to it later and you will understand. I am way off the track and not doing my job of emptying this entire storage closet, but each piece of fabric I pull out of the trunk starts a new reel. We went back to Washington after Prague to a house we bought in Chevy Chase across the street from Lyndon Johnson's friend and close crony, Walter Jenkins, who brought disgrace to his family for doing something reprehensible in the men's room of the YMCA. I could look it up in the archives of the *Washington Post*. It was all over the newspapers at the time, but I don't care enough now. I have finished grieving for Walter Jenkins' five children. They moved back to Texas after that, and we didn't hear anything more. As far as Washington was concerned, it became a non-event almost overnight.

CHAPTER ONE
The Chicago Kiss

WHEN ALBERT FINALLY CAME HOME after completing his thirty missions in the Central Pacific with the 7th Air Force, he was adorned with medals and looked even more appealing to me than ever. Nevertheless, I was still too shy or unsure of myself or wary to let him know it. My greeting, known as "the Chicago kiss," was a bone of contention all the rest of our lives together. He thought it not sufficiently demonstrative for the occasion, and I thought it quite appropriate. That stage passed quickly and I was eager to be married as soon as the Air Force would give him leave, which is the way it finally happened. I worked my shift at the hospital until the day before the wedding.

The war lasted one more year, during which there was always the vague threat that Albert would be reassigned overseas for another tour, although the Air Force had promised that would not happen. He had talked a lot about the Foreign Service, which I encouraged him to pursue, not only because I knew he would be a great diplomat but also because it would be a profession I could share, since at heart I am an actress.

He decided to give it a try. But first he had to study.

After four years in the Air Force concentrating on surviving air battles, he rightly declared that he had lost track of what was going on in the great big world. So after he was released we sought refuge in his family's summer cottage in Michigan to cram. I was the messenger and cook, shuffling back and forth to the library at Hope College in Holland, Michigan, bringing him study materials, visiting the grocery store, and my doctor. I was pregnant by then and doing well. This combination of simple jobs somehow made me very content. After three months it was time to face the music, so we stayed with my parents in Chicago while he took the grueling test, a written one in those days, six hours for each of two days.

The exams were corrected by hand, so the waiting period before we heard would be long. We had to do something to earn a living, so we went to Grand Rapids, Michigan, where there was a place for a clerk in the offices of three ancient gentlemen and a junior partner who had not been in the service because he'd had polio as a youth. The three elderly gentlemen were brave, since they employed at that time two ex-servicemen both with law degrees but no previous record of practice. The two were Albert W. Sherer, Jr., and Gerald R. Ford.

When word finally came that Bud had passed the written exam, it was time to go back into isolation in the country to study French, because there would be a foreign language section on the oral exam. When we left at the end of the traditional farewell party - paper cups half-filled with warm wine - I remember Jerry's saying, "I have a hunch we'll meet again. I feel Washington calling me."

I could help a lot with the French study because I had learned the language well at the boarding school I had gone to up in New Hampshire before attending college. There had been nothing to do at boarding school but ski and study, and we had a real French woman as an avid teacher. I was almost constantly assigned to the French table in the dining room, which I did not appreciate at all, until many years later when my knowledge of the language saved our lives. I had no idea it had been permanently imbedded in my brain.

The morning of the exam Albert telephoned from Washington and said, all stuffed up, "I think I'm dying." Together we worked on a scenario which went something like this:

Examiner (in French): "Good morning. How are you?"

Albert (all stuffed up, in French): "Sorry I have a little cold."

The examiner was very sympathetic and asked fewer questions. Among the other queries put to him was one Bud couldn't answer in any language – (in French), "Why did we have sugar rationing in the United States during the war when Cuba (our friend at the time) was so close and had plenty of sugar?"

Bud had to reply (in French), "Sorry, Sir, I don't know."

Well, he passed nonetheless, and we pondered that question the rest of our lives.

Our son, Peter, was born soon after, so I stayed in my parents' summer place while Bud went to Washington to find out why he had heard nothing yet from the State Department. They said in the most matter-of-fact way, "Oh, well, yes. You are scheduled to start training in three days." Eventually I guess we accustomed ourselves to surprises. It was an important survival weapon.

At the conclusion of the training I was in perfect shape

again and hurried to Washington to hear the news. I already knew it included an assignment as an "Unclassified" Foreign Service Officer to Tangier, Morocco, which I had to find on a map. My education must have been deficient in geography, a characteristic I now believe to have been universal in the United States, then and now.

It was in Washington, on the terrace of the Shoreham Hotel, that I met Francis E. Meloy, Albert's best friend from their class at the Foreign Service School. The two remained best friends for the rest of Fran's life, which ended suddenly in 1976 when he was Ambassador to Lebanon where he was kidnapped and murdered by the PLO. Fran's first assignment was to Bahrain, Saudi Arabia, which he later described as nothing but a sea of sand and a lot of oil wells. Before we left for our first posts, we went to New York with Fran to have what we later called a "whing-ding," and which we repeated as often as possible in various other places over the years. We went for a hansom cab ride in the Park, dined at 21 and then went to the Stork Club to drink some more and dance until the early morning. We spent the night at the Plaza, got up luxuriously late and finished our splurge at Rumplemeyer's where we had what is nowadays called brunch, but we didn't know that word then.

CHAPTER TWO

A White Feather Hat

AFTER CAREFULLY READING THE POST REPORT provided by the State Department and being injected for dis-
eases I had not thought of encountering close-up in my
lifetime, we started out with thirteen pieces of baggage,
including our baby, Peter, who traveled in a wicker basket
covered by a mosquito net. He was by that time three
months old, thoroughly healthy, happy and lots of fun. I
was making my first trip to Europe, so I dressed in a manner I thought appropriate, including high-heeled blue
shoes and a white feather hat, both very fashionable at the
time. I looked wonderful.

It was 1946, and so soon after the termination of World
War II that very little on either side of the Atlantic Ocean
had been restored to its previous condition. This included
the vessel that carried us to Le Havre. She was an uncon-
verted troop transport from the war with dormitories seg-
regated by sex and equipped with hammocks. Our baby
saved us. We were assigned a small cabin with bunk beds
because we had the youngest passenger on board. The
hammocks caused most of our Foreign Service friends aim-
ing for Madrid to sleep on deck most nights. We sat with

them at our assigned table in the dining room where we were offered by our jolly waiter either "cow juice" or water. There was no bar on board, probably a good thing, although at the time it seemed cruel punishment. Peter's regular formula was made from a product called Dextrimaltose mixed with evaporated milk. Enough of those ingredients had been included in a footlocker which was supposed to be put in our cabin but had been loaded into the hold by mistake... So my hero was obliged to go to the ship's kitchen each day to prepare the formula from something the chef provided. I don't know what. The child was already rugged, I guess, because no negative effects were noticed.

The crossing took ten days. As we approached the shore of France, I got my first look at what war damage could be. Our Air Force had bombed the harbor so thoroughly that when we landed and went ashore, the only way was down a skinny wooden ramp from the level of the third deck wearing my high-heeled shoes and the white feather hat. Albert managed the baby in his basket and I, holding my breath all the way down, managed myself.

We took the boat train to Paris where, by that time, it was not only dark but cold and raining. There were no taxis, so we stood on the street corner a long time, Peter in his basket on the pavement shielded by his father's coat. The white feather hat must have looked especially appealing by that time. Finally, after hailing every passing vehicle, we were saved by an American soldier in a jeep. He took us to the embassy, located in the same place it is today. Albert was more than a little choleric when the clerk could find no record of us in the books. Finally he managed to find one room for us in the Hotel Mont Tabor on the street of that name. We were grateful, even though the place had no heat, no hot water, and no food. The army sergeant at the embassy gave Albert chits that we could use at an army mess nearby. Peter's diet was not in jeopardy because we had recaptured the missing footlocker on the dock. We stayed in that bedraggled hotel for about a week, feeling lucky that we had a roof over our heads and the gourmet food at the mess hall. While we were out, Peter was looked after by Jeanne, the sad cook of the hotel who had nothing to cook. One evening when we came in from dinner I found a pretty little Catholic medal pinned to Peter's nightgown. I kept it and, every now and then, I hold it in my hand and remember....

We finally caught on to the system of acquiring rail tickets in a reasonable length of time. It was a simple transaction between the station master and Albert. As soon as Albert produced the required number of cartons of Winston cigarettes, the tickets were provided, good for travel all the way to Madrid. So we were on our way.

The window of the compartment, which we shared with four or five other travelers, had to be left open because, as the day progressed, it got hotter and hotter. Lumps of coal blew in and settled on Peter's mosquito netting. I hadn't been a "mère de famille" for very long and feared this would have some undesirable consequences, but no one noticed. The other occupants of the compartment just kept smiling. So I had to smile back.

Finally we stopped at the last town in France, a place called Hendaye. The passengers had thinned out along the way, and we were the only ones left in our compartment. The conductor came along and told us, to our amazement, that we were at the end of the line. We explained that we had tickets all the way to Madrid, but he said the border was closed and we would have to find some other way of getting across. So we got out of the train as instructed. A porter helped unload the thirteen pieces of baggage and we went in to the little station to figure out how to proceed and try to find a snack. Both these purposes were accomplished fairly quickly because by magic there appeared a donkey cart with a driver eager to drive us on. So once again the luggage was loaded, I sat in the cart on a suitcase holding "le meilleur baggage" as our third passenger became known. The ride was lumpy but short. Albert walked by the side while the driver explained that he could take us only "to the middle of the bridge". I didn't think of it at the time, but I wish I had taken a photograph of our family crossing for a Christmas card. "C'est le pont qui est la frontière entre la France et l'Espagne," we were informed in the most matter-of-fact way by our chauffeur. "Il faut traverser la frontière à pied."

It was more easily said than done, what with the footlocker and all, but we made several trips slowly and were greeted by a crew of very sullen border guards who wouldn't have been welcoming in any case because we hadn't allowed them to win the war and they were still mad about that. Finally, a taxi turned up, and we were taken to the station in Irun, the Spanish border town where, with the same old tickets that had brought us all the way from Paris, we boarded a train for Madrid. We were met by a car from the embassy, heavy reinforcement of the fact that we really were in the Foreign Service and somebody besides us knew it. This wonderful car took us to the Ritz Hotel. Need I say more? Only one additional train ride, and a ferry across the Straits of Gibralter lay between us and our destination.

On the ferry we finally saw the green hills of Tangier in the distance and had a good whiff of the raw garlic and the fresh oranges, which were the Spanish prescription for sea-sickness. With my white feather hat in place, we were ready to debark. The entire American staff of the Legation was there to greet us. Albert knew some of them because all except one were Yale men, a homogeneous group that you would not find today, and a fact that tells you something. It was a long time ago.

CHAPTER THREE

Smugglers and Other Miscreants

T HE CITY WAS FULL OF SMUGGLERS and other miscreants. Being a true international city, they had an open money market, meaning that currency from any country could be changed at any time of the day to the foreign currency of any other country. This provided unlimited opportunities for laundering. And there was plenty of dirty linen. The Americans had their own consular court. According to the mythology, it was created during the presidency of Teddy Roosevelt who sent a battleship to Tangier to rescue an American citizen who had been kidnapped by a pirate. "Perdicaris alive or Raisuli dead" was the war cry. Any number of Americans were saved by that consular court in our time, mostly GI's who had stayed there after the war and were making a handsome living driving excess U.S. Army equipment across the border and selling it for large sums to buyers from all over the world. And they got into all sorts of trouble. Albert, since he was the only lawyer on the staff, was the Judge of that court. He found it a challenging assignment and scary because there was no recourse from the court short of the Supreme Court of the United States. If there were a murder, what would he do?

Perhaps it was there that he honed his considerable diplomatic skills and his remarkable talent for persuasion, which served him well all of the rest of his life.

We stayed in a hotel for about three months. (Everything cooked in unrefined olive oil. Have you ever tasted it? If not, please don't go out of your way.) We finally found a house, albeit without hot running water, but we knew we were lucky to get out of the hotel and start to live. I had already hired a nursemaid to look after Peter because no mercy was shown on the question of making the necessary diplomatic calls. I was required to put on my white gloves and make a call on everyone in the diplomatic corps who outranked me and that meant everyone. Accompanying me through this baptism of fire was Julia Goodyear, wife of the second in command of our Legation. She was a very intelligent Smith graduate, and I came to enjoy these visits very much. The women I met were interesting, sophisticated people whom Julia knew quite well. I didn't say anything that I remember except once. The Portugese Consul's wife, a pretty young woman, said in French, "Julia, we have been transferred to Boston and I am worried." That seemed like a *non sequitur* to me, but she went on to add, "I am pregnant, which makes me worry. Is it possible to find a good doctor there? And a hospital?"

It was obvious that she thought the place was most likely inhabited by wild Indians or gangsters. I was so shocked that instantly I blurted out, "Boston is a city famous for its medical facilities and, in fact, I have a brother who is right now in Boston training to be a surgeon. If you like, I will give you his name so you will have a connection to the best." She thanked me but she never asked me to do anything for her. I tell this vignette because that was the moment I woke up to the fact that what I had considered cruel and unusual punishment at boarding school - namely vigorous French language study - could help me solve real problems. My confidence in my ability to cope in this strange place took a giant leap forward.

The house we finally rented consisted of a living room, dining room and kitchen downstairs. It must have been built as a summer place because the only heat source was a tiny fireplace in the corner of the living room, where we huddled for the next three winters. There were no closets in the house, which shouldn't have been a surprise because looking around should have told me that Moroccans don't need to hang up their clothes. Through the Legation I found "Jesus", a master carpenter and dead ringer for the pictures in my Sunday school books. There were lovely Spanish style tiles on all the floors, beautiful but cold. Among our personal effects was a set of the Encyclopedia Britannica which had to be put somewhere in a house with not one shelf, so I designed a resting place for them under a bay window in the living room which doubled as a window seat with a cushion on it made from one of the fabrics I remembered during the excavation of the trunk. The single bathroom had a small tub, which we filled with ten inches of cold water, adding a couple of kettles of boiling water from the tank on the side of the wood-burning stove where all the cooking was done. Laundry was done in a big cauldron set in the back yard over a tripod. Finally I had a twenty-five gallon hot water heater sent from Sears Roebuck, which helped a lot for baths, even though it frequently blew out all the fuses in the house. Electricity and water were a constant problem. Descriptions of Iraq today remind me of it. Both utilities were sporadic during the day creating a housekeeping problem we had to learn to live with.

The Spanish Moroccan cook I hired lasted a year or so, but she had such sticky fingers that I finally had to fire her and take on a Moroccan. Halima was a very good cook but when she lost her temper and went after the indispensable nanny with a butcher knife, I had to let her go. Her successor, cook number three, also a Moroccan, turned out to be the mildest, sweetest woman I met during the years we were there. When my parents came to visit, she invited all of us to her house for a real Moroccan dinner. That was a gesture of friendship that I encountered from no one else.

We had gone with our friend Fran Meloy to a wholesale food vendor in New York to order peanut butter and other specialties we knew we would not find at our respective destinations. So we counseled each other from a base of total ignorance about what would be needed in our new places of residence. Eventually when our shipment arrived I got "Jesus" to build shelves in a tiny room next to the kitchen in which I stored everything I wanted to save and from then on I went around all day long with keys in my pocket. That became part of my professional life that lasted to the end. I never got accustomed to it.

Very soon after we were installed in our new surroundings, a sad, freak accident caused turmoil in our lives, which seemed to be composed of one shock after another. An airplane crash in the Rif Mountains killed the wife and daughter of the new U.S. Consul General assigned to Casablanca as well as a vice-consul on his way to his new assignment. The Consul General, who had stayed behind in Paris for further briefings, arrived two days later to face this terrible news. When the Minister in Tangier technically responsible for the Consulate in Casa asked his staff whether anyone was acquainted with the Consul General, only Bud raised his hand. He had met Howard Elting casually in Washington where both were preparing for service in Morocco. So it was decided that the Sherers would go to Casablanca to assist in any way they could at the time of the funeral. I never knew whether Howard was aware that we were there, the extent of his shock was so extreme.

The State Department said right away that Howard would be free to depart from his post any time he chose, but he firmly refused the offer because, after all, his family was buried there, and he needed to stay. A couple of months later, it was decided that Bud should go down there to assist in the office and live in the official residence of the Consul General with Howard. Fate could not have ordained a better person for that touchy job. Bud's instincts and gentle nature were exactly what was required to wean Howard away from daily visits to the cemetery and a dozen other symptoms that indicated that he had not even begun to let go. The child's bicycle was finally removed from the front hall.

In the meantime, the wife of the young Vice-Consul who was killed in the plane crash had stayed in Evanston, Illinois, with her family. Because she had a brand new baby, she had decided to let her husband go ahead to find them a place to live. Eventually she had gone to Washington and taken a job in the State Department. When Howard finally returned there after two years, he felt he had to see her immediately since he knew all the details firsthand of where her husband was buried and how. So, being the grand gentleman he was, he telephoned her on the first day and invited her to lunch. Later the story was that they had dinner together that same day and decided that the only logical scenario was that they should marry as soon as possible. It worked. Her son had a father and Howard had a family. We remained close and loyal friends, all five of us, for the rest of our lives.

CHAPTER FOUR

Babies and Other Surprises

Our house came with its gardener, Mohamed, who lived with his son, Abdel Kadir, in a shack in our garden. He grew vegetables for the house. I remember tiny artichokes, the blossoms of thistle bushes, which we ate whole. They had a purple cast like the artichokes I had known. Also there was sorrel, a green leafy vegetable that tasted like spinach with lemon juice on it, delicious. (Later I tried taking seeds home to our summer place in Michigan, where they refused to take hold.) Hamed tended the burro we eventually bought for Peter and went every morning to the market to buy fresh bread for all of us. When Peter was old enough, he rode on "Mokey" to fetch the bread, an important daily outing for all three of them. Hamed was accustomed to foreigners and seemed impervious to the odd behavior and customs sometimes practiced by his employers. He was gentle and smiley and always willing. His son worked at the printing press owned and operated by the proprietor of our house. He, too, was gentle, remarkably more sophisticated than his father. I say that only because his command of French and Spanish was superior to that of other Moors with the exception of the educated politicians we came to know. We saw Abdel Kadir very little, and I always wondered where he went on weekends and other times when he was not working. Eventually he moved away somewhere because Hamed decided he needed a wife.

As far as we could tell, Hamed paid an agent to find Fatima, a sum we gave him as a wedding present. She arrived by taxi, suffering from a headache because, as it was explained to me, it was her first ride in an automobile, and she found it nerve-wracking. I acquired this information through Antoinette, the Spanish Moroccan nanny, whom I sent to Hamed's house shortly after Fatima's arrival to find out if everything was all right. We provided aspirin, which was gratefully received and reported to be effective. Soon she was employed as a cleaning person and laundress in the house and all odd jobs were assigned to her. She spoke only Arabic so there were the inevitable minor disasters. I remember the day I thought the kitten I had picked up in the market when I was on a routine price-checking tour was ready to try the out-of-doors for the first time. I asked Fatima to take the kitten outside thinking, of course, that she would bring it back. Fatima, however, understood that I didn't want it any more so she took it way out into a eucalyptus forest and abandoned it. I was sorry and so was she, but my miserable Arabic was what it was - primitive.

During the years that followed, I often used Antoinette as a translator and adviser. Although she had a tremendous Spanish temper, she was the luckiest find I ever had. Soon I was pregnant again, and she was not only capable but willing to take care of two babies, a monumental task given the limitations of our domicile and facilities. To her they seemed more than adequate, even grand, and the security we could offer of plenty to eat and a comfortable room, I guess, made the demanding work worthwhile. Besides, she eventually became so devoted to the children that the arguments we often had, she and I, were almost always over something to do with their care, like whether she was giving one of them too much Denticina, a powder used as the solution to all problems connected with teething. I had no way of knowing the composition of this treatment, but it seemed to work, and it satisfied Antoinette that the children were getting the best treatment, so I went along.

I elected to stay in Tangier to deliver the second baby, which of course was of concern to my parents; but I had no enthusiasm for the picture of leaving my husband for an extended period of time and traveling alone with a newborn. I chose the British missionary hospital, a small facility located in a typical villa painted white and surrounded by well-tended gardens where the good Dr. Anderson took me on as a patient. I soon learned how to count my weight in stones, but otherwise there seemed little difference from my previous experience, which was still fresh in my mind.

The part that was truly unique was the drama of the delivery. In the afternoon of the day I felt the baby was coming, I telephoned Dr. Anderson to give him some advance notice. "Well, good," he said, "wait awhile and call me again later." This short and strange conversation was repeated several times until it got to be about seven o'clock in the evening. Bud decided we should not call any more, so I took the small suitcase I had prepared and waited in the car, while he went out to tell the doctor we were there. I waited a long time. I think it was a long time. It felt like a long time. Finally Bud came out and told me that we could go in, things were ready. "Can you walk?" he asked. "We are going into the nurses' home which is next door."

I was not in a mood by then to wonder much about that. I flew out of the car and into the front door of Hope House, where a bed had been prepared in a room right next to the door. From then on, everything went smoothly. I found out at last why in literature and movies there are always newspapers on the bed when a baby is being born. I also found out what chloroform is like. My lasting impression is that it is splendid. Or, now that I think of it, maybe they gave me what we used to call "laughing gas" because I remember vividly that I giggled through the whole show. There I was with a little mask over my nose and mouth and a bulb in my hand. The instructions were to squeeze the bulb every time I felt a pain that I judged to be outrageous. I did that and it worked! For my trouble they handed me a mini redheaded girl named Susan. She was a year younger than her brother, a lucky statistic that made life much simpler in the ensuing years. They were not only exceptionally compatible from the beginning, but later on they traveled together, alleviating somewhat their parents' major attacks of anxiety.

During that first night in Hope House, I wondered why the nurses had left the door of my room open when there was a large English grandfather clock just outside the door which counted not only the hours but the half and quarter hours. Even after producing a baby, my exhaustion level was not high enough to keep me asleep. The explanation was shared with me only a couple of days later when Albert told me that the medical people and the holy people had quarreled at the last minute about whether it was correct for Dr. Anderson to admit me to the hospital. The holy people contended that they were all out there expressly to serve the local population and nobody else. The medical people had argued that the Europeans paid real money, which was always in short supply, so it didn't make sense not to admit them when an opportunity came along. Their concession finally was that they would put me in Hope House instead of in the hospital itself. But the holy people were not satisfied, and when I had telephoned to say that I was ready to come, the key to the room prepared for me was nowhere to be found.

It was after Bud and I arrived needing immediate help that he and Dr. Anderson broke the door down with their shoulders. When I finally heard the story, I understood why the grandfather clock had been so bothersome. And that's why I have never really approved of missionaries who have conversions as their primary goal.

While I was a patient at Hope House, Bud found an ad in the *Tangier Gazette* for an auction at the home of Mrs. Verdon, an elderly English lady who was liquidating her household effects because she had decided to move permanently to England. She was well-known in the foreign community, the widow of a doctor who had been personal physician to the Sultan for many years. Bud thought she might have a chest of drawers we could use to contain our new baby's not-very-vast wardrobe. When he came the next day to report on this important quest, he said, "It was wonderful. I bought two muskets."

I was appropriately surprised.

"But the real adventure came when I got them home and Hamed came to the car as usual to help me unload. One look at what I had in the car and he turned on his heels and went to his house without saying a word."

I knew he had never behaved that way before. "Did you find out what was wrong?"

Finally it came out. Hamed had been Dr. Verdon's gun bearer when he was a boy and apparently for a number of years after. He had polished and tended and revered those muskets, which had been a gift to the good doctor from the Sultan himself, and Hamed thought some sort of skullduggery must have taken place in order for the sainted guns to land in the hands of a foreigner and an infidel. When it was explained that Mrs. Verdon herself had sold them and that we would revere them all the more for knowing that they had at one time been near and dear to Hamed, all was finally forgiven and forgotten.

The Sultan of Morocco, regarded by foreigners as a figurehead, although an important one, paid one unforgettable visit to Tangier while we were there, causing much excitement and elaborate preparations. Streets were cleaned and flowers in the parks and along the route he would travel from the train station were beefed up. We had an ideal vantage point from which to observe his arrival with a harem said to number forty women, a number of beautiful Arabian horses, and of course a retinue of staff. Our perch was the second story of a colleague's house, which was next door to the Mendoubia, residence of the Sultan's representative in Tangier. A large vehicle looking rather like a house trailer backed up to the gates of the Mendoubia from which the women were discharged into the palace without being shown to the outside world. We, however, could see them as they emerged onto the roof garden of the Mendoubia to stretch their legs and breathe some fresh air. They were dressed like fairy-tale oriental women or maybe that is my warped recollection, diaphanous gowns and ropes of gold jewelry. It must have been thrilling to go on a trip. They giggled and whispered together like schoolgirls.

The Sultan's official residence was Fez. The French kept him on a very tight leash, always fearing, I suppose, that he had enough power among the people to initiate an uprising against them. During the celebrations in honor of the Sultan's visit we were invited to an official dinner at the French Embassy, where I was seated next to the Pasha of Marrakesh, who wore a dagger at his waist positioned in perfect line with my thigh. Managing to retrieve my power of speech I asked him about the rings on his fingers. On that occasion they were huge emeralds, and he hesitated not an instant to explain to me that his precious stones were kept in drawers in his living quarters so he could choose his adornments easily. He did not appear to be a man who kidded around much. With his neatly trimmed beard and his brown complexion and his dagger in its silver and gold sheath he was formidable. I hadn't met a pasha before. We didn't have those in Chicago.

We soon discovered that one of the duties of a vice-consul was to witness the weddings of American citizens and issue signed marriage certificates. There was a certain Reverend Grosholtz, a Christian fundamentalist, who, for a fee, was willing to marry any couples who came along. What proof the candidates had that they were not already married to someone else or that a divorce was final was never clear, but when the Reverend called, we responded. I assumed that he must have been checked by the authorities or he would not have been on an approved list. It was odd, however, that the couples were invariably middle-aged, usually over for a weekend from Rome or Madrid, and never came to be married in the Catholic Church. The Good Reverend Grosholtz had composed his own remarkable wedding service. I remember little of the details, except that he addressed the bride as "rib", exacting strict promises of fealty, while I sat at his air pedal organ attempting to play appropriate music and not laugh. It was a tough job. I might add that these ceremonies were held in an open-air chapel he had probably constructed himself. I never knew whether he actually had a congregation, but I suspect not. He was dedicated to the marrying business in his retirement years.

The vice-consuls sometimes had extremely touchy problems to unravel. I remember the female sailor who appeared in Bud's office one evening casting a large spooky shadow over his desk. It was late, and no secretary was on duty. He judged by the girth of her biceps that she could make pulp out of him in short order if she chose. He was extra attentive to her story. Her name was Doris.

"Are you a consul or something?" she bellowed.

"Yes. What can I do for you?"

She declined the offer of a chair. "You can get me out of this damned place, that's what!" She wanted access to an American vessel that would take her back to the States by giving her employment as a crewmember. She was a bona fide member of the Longshoremen's Union and had a union card and an American passport to prove it. She had come up from Port Lyautey, a port of call for numerous American vessels on the coast near Casablanca. She had been working there as a prostitute attempting for months to hitch a ride, but no captain would accept her. She had no money to pay for any accommodations while she waited, so the vice-consul had to find a source.

What Albert found was a fund administered by the local chapter of the American Red Cross, which had been created from contributions donated over a period of years at a special Thanksgiving Day service at the little Anglican Church. The money was to be used for the benefit of indigent American citizens should any needy persons turn up. The keeper of this fund was the delicate, very proper French wife of the American Chief of Mission. She did not respond with enthusiasm to the idea that her fund be used for the upkeep of a prostitute. But Doris fit the description perfectly of persons for whom the fund was intended and her husband, our Chief, wished to get rid of this albatross as quickly as possible. So Doris was installed in a moderate hotel and instructed by the vice-consul that practicing her trade would kill the deal. By that time there was a vice-consul even more low-ranking than Bud. Every time an American vessel dropped anchor, it was his job to put Doris in a boat and row out to the oceangoing ship, shouting up, "Ahoy, there, an American seaman coming aboard!" You don't know the vice-consul and I'm not going to record his name although it would make the story even more surreal because he had a sissy-sounding name. Suffice it to say that he eventually succeeded in his mission but not in the Foreign Service.

CHAPTER FIVE

Half a Century Later
A Few Things Change

Beyond the never-ending diplomatic parties there was little formal entertainment except what we created for ourselves, like the theater productions at the little theater in the basement of the property used by the British Council as a library and information center. The plays, enjoyed by everyone in the foreign community, were mostly English, and great attention was given to costumes and scenery. Given the limited sources of diversion at the time, these plays were lifesavers. I acted in many of them, a source of great enjoyment and camaraderie at a time when I needed it.

There was one other diversion. We would spend the occasional evening at the Parade Bar run by two Americans. It was the gathering place for the young literati, a group which comprised a number of twentieth-century geniuses. There was Paul Bowles, who stayed in Tangier until his death in 1999 and his mixed-up wife Jane. Jane was mostly stretched out on a banquette with a girlfriend, both appearing to be half out of it on drugs or alcohol or both. Sometimes we greeted each other but mostly she was too preoccupied. Then there was Truman Capote and William Burroughs. Others, such as Tennessee Williams, came and went. Tangier was the place to be at that time if you wanted to be where "anything goes".

Times have changed. I spent several days in the city with Susan as a present (I think it was more a present for me) on her 50th birthday in 1997 and managed to peek down a dingy side street where I spotted the Parade Bar securely boarded up. We noticed that William Burroughs is buried in the graveyard at the Anglican Church, the only physical reminder we saw of the carefree, bygone days. The cafes and restaurants were filled with men only all day long, chatting in a desultory way and smoking. On the other hand, however, the shop windows displayed garments at least as fetching as "Victoria's Secret," and there were fewer veiled women than I remembered and even a couple of girls in blue jeans.

The most gratifying adventure on that trip was visiting the interior of the very house where we had lived, Susan's first home. Diligent persistence was required for us to find it, after a 50-year absence. The name of the street has been changed from Calle Vasco da Gama to Avenue des Ecosses (no logical explanation for that, not even revolutionary spite) and another house has been built on the land that was our garden, so it doesn't look the same from the street.

We had a guide whom we had engaged through our hotel, but he was of little use – too young for institutional memory. But we had luck in the form of a beautifully attired Moorish gentleman wearing a clean white djellaba with a hand-woven, turquoise-colored sash around the waist and a matching band around his wide-brimmed straw hat. He was carrying a basket, which made me think he lived in the neighborhood and was on his way to the market. We stopped him and asked in French if he remembered an English lady who lived up the narrow cobbled lane going up the hill at the side of our house. "Oh yes," he said, switching immediately into English, "you mean Mrs. Greene." I was getting excited because I knew already that we were in the right place. The gentleman was excited too and continued, "And Puti?"

Now I was certain. Puti was the coal-black servant, guardian, business manager, nurse and cook for Ada Greene. He was a beautiful man whom she had brought from Sudan after the days when Mr. Greene was the British governor of that colony. As far as I could see (and I went to Ada often for advice and comfort), Puti was her entire support system. She was always stretched out on her divan-chaise longue with a long pastel-colored chiffon scarf wrapped around her head and neck, which completely disguised any loose skin or wrinkles that were undoubtedly lurking in that area. All that showed was a frame of pure white hair around her wonderful bony face. She had a colorful parrot in a cage next to her who butted in to the conversation once in a while. And she was never without her signature cigarette holder, which in my memory was one foot long. I will look like Ada when I get old, one of many unkept promises to myself.

So it was Ada, long gone, who came to my rescue once again.

"Yes, your house is still there. Walk up this road to the first gate on the right and ring the bell. The owner is a nice person."

I wanted to throw my arms around the gentleman's neck but I managed to restrain myself and we bid a proper

farewell. Then Susan and I started up the hill followed by
our useless guide. I was wondering whether the Berber
women carrying large bundles of faggots on their backs,
ululating as they went to keep their spirits up, were still at
it. The solid steel gate was not far away, but since we could
not see through it, I had no preview. I rang the bell and
waited impatiently until a servant came to open up. I
explained that we had once lived there and would like to
have a look inside. She gave no sign of having understood
anything I said and closed the gate slowly as though indeed
something more might happen. And it did. In a few minutes the proprietor himself opened up and when he heard
our story, he proudly invited us in.

Yes, it was the place, much enlarged and fancified. I had
a choking wave of nostalgia for my young husband, but
curiosity took over when the owner stepped back to let us
in. A more impressive entry door had been added, but I
soon oriented myself. The corner fireplace in the living
room appeared to be out of service, since the furniture
arranged Arab style around the periphery of the room side
by side had placed two enormous armchairs directly in
front of it. I wondered afterwards whether it was now a sitting room for ladies, since a much bigger and imposing
room had been added on the left of what used to be the
front door, at the end of the façade. Soon a grandmother
appeared, a smiley, gracious lady dressed all in black as
though she might have been a servant but obviously was
not as she proudly joined us on our tour of the house. I
managed not to say, "I assume you have hot running water
now" as we saw one bathroom after another, all in exotic
colors. I remember particularly one in which the appliances
were the color of the bougainvillea at the front door, dark

shocking pink, and there was another in shiny black. The best part of the tour was finding the room Susan and Peter had shared unchanged. My mind's eye furnished it with two Kiddie-Koops, cribs that were fashionable at the time when they were babies, screened sort of cages even over the tops, a perfect solution to the bug problem. I don't remember that we had many insects, but new mothers can imagine all sorts of things.

After the tour we were invited to sit in a parlor, which had been our dining room, where we had no difficulty making animated conversation with the owner, and where the grandmother served delicious mint tea and stale French biscuits. Pretty soon two handsome young boys came bouncing into the room. They had just returned from the French school dressed in the traditional navy blue short pants and jackets with white shirts. On command they shook our hands and gave that little bow which is as French as the clothes they were wearing. I was hoping that the mother would show up, but it was explained that the driver was now on his way to pick her up after a meeting. We were loath to take up any more of their day although there was no indication that Dad needed to get back to his desk.

So we took our leave, slowly. They made us promise that on a return visit to their city we would visit them again. I have thought many times about that day in 1997, having strong doubts that in my lifetime an experience like that can be repeated. Doors don't open readily any more, especially to Americans.

CHAPTER SIX

A Lot to Learn and Tough Choices to Make

THREE YEARS SPED BY. Then a telegram from the State Department: "Would we like to go to Madagascar?"

"No", we replied. It seemed like more of the same. We had had enough dysentery for the time being. I was down to one hundred pounds.

"What about Calcutta?" was the next query.

I wasn't keen but we both knew there was a lot to learn in India so we said "OK".

I left Tangier as soon as I could with the children, thinking we could all get the necessary immunizations and do some shopping for tropical wear and still have time for a leisurely vacation seeing all our family before taking off again. This left Albert all alone with our poodle but not for too long. He followed along soon after by ferry to Gibraltar, where he was refused entry because in the British Territories then people importing pets were required to leave them in quarantine for six months before they could be admitted as permanent residents. Doubtless there was a temporary kennel at the dock, but for some reason he chose not to submit his dog to such an indignity. The only alternative was to rent a rowboat and row around, the two of them, for three hours in the Straits of Gibralter until they were invited to board their ocean-going vessel. It was July. The sun was hot, and Albert was wearing his best suit.

Everything I know about India to this day is what I learned from the reading I did during that period between Tangier and learning that the assignment had suddenly been changed to Budapest, probably while Albert was on the high seas in the rowboat. It was explained that the Legal Attaché at the Legation there had died and when the State Department searched their roster for available replacements with law degrees, only one name popped up. That assignment, I see now, determined in one way or another everything that happened to us in the Foreign Service later. We weren't thinking, for the moment, of that or much of anything else as we romped around New York on another celebratory whing-ding with our friend Fran Meloy who was just back from Dharan, Saudi Arabia. As we walked in to the 21 Club lobby, there was a television set, a device we had only read about.

"Well," one of us said, "that must be television."

Somebody else said, "That can't be television because they're playing baseball and it's dark out."

Just then, Charlie Krindel owner of 21, appeared at our elbow. "Say," he said, "where are you fellas from?" When he heard replies to that question, we all shook hands, and he said he would like to give us dinner on the house. Fran ordered a tureen (silver, he specified) of spinach. Bud had corn (from Michigan, he specified) and I had a platter of smoked salmon. I remember every bite. Drinks were also on the house and we had a few before going on to the Stork Club.

In the fall of 1949 we sailed for Rotterdam safely protected from cholera, bubonic plague, and yellow fever. We had our car on board, so we drove through Germany, an awesome experience. The devastation I had seen in Paris three years earlier seemed mild compared with what had happened in Nurnberg and Dresden. My mother used to refer often to the time she went to Dresden to study dance with Mary Wigman, a pioneer in modern dance in the early 30's. I knew vaguely about the famous art museum, and I knew about Dresden china, but that was all. I learned later that what I saw there, which spread all over the only navigable street, was the remainder of one of the greatest modern cities of Europe.

Over the years we had many chances to see Nurnberg "come to" and develop into a stronger and certainly more beautiful city than it had been even in Hitler's time. The U.S. Army took over a large German hospital and made it larger so in our Eastern European posts we had that safety valve which was a comfort. Our food came from the Army Commissary, as did most of the rest of what we consumed. Nonetheless, we depended on the local market when our little Legation in Budapest ran out of stock, and we learned to eat some new comestibles like frog legs (delicious) and brains and kidneys (also delicious). The city had, like the rest of Europe, suffered considerable damage during the war caused by the bombing of the U.S. Air Force. Hungary had been part of the Austro-Hungarian Empire, which of course put it in the German camp. At the time we arrived, there was only one bridge over the Danube, plus a pontoon bridge built by the Army when it had come through.

We found a house, which, like the Tangier house, had been built as a summer residence. It was heated only by large porcelain stoves, the kind you see when you tour French chateaux. They were real works of art, those stoves, although never efficient enough to make anyone feel really cozy. The stoves were wood burning, tended in our house by Feribaci (Uncle Francis), a relative of the two glamorous sisters who owned the house. He came into our bedroom every morning carrying the wood to stoke the fire wearing one of his beautiful shirts trimmed by his baron's coronet on the pocket. We were still in bed. He greeted us not exactly cheerily but amiably and went about his work. Feribaci was diabetic so by supplying him with insulin, which he administered himself, I could help him a little. He had a room in our basement, which I never saw, as he had been living there before we moved in. He was glad to have food and shelter and whatever income we provided. He seemed very old to me. He never smiled.

One of the glamorous sisters, always known as "Bebi" (pronounced "baby"), lived with her husband and five-year-old son in the gardener's cottage at the bottom of a hill behind our house. The other one, always called "Nuni", lived in an apartment in the city with her husband. The Communists had been elected shortly before we arrived in 1950, so these upper-class young men were considered lucky to have jobs at all, even though everyone thought the political situation could not last long. People imagined that the government would certainly collapse as soon as the population realized what they had done. In fact, it was 1956 before there was an uprising, which liberated many, including most of the young friends we made during the time we lived in that picturesque house, but by that time we were long gone.

Right away after moving into the house we started giving wonderful parties with gypsy orchestras and plenty of good food and drink brought in from the PX in Vienna. The sisters, with whom we became good friends, introduced us to a crowd of charming young people who were very frank about the conditions that were being imposed on them, so it was a good way for Albert to become aware of opinions at least in a small segment of the population. We were very naïve then in not imagining that some of our guests were reporting to the secret police. The other guests were equally naïve in accepting our invitations.

An American businessman was arrested and accused of anti-state activities. He was kept in prison for nine months and then testified that there had been a plot to overthrow the government that involved Albert Sherer along with nine other individuals including Archbishop Grosz, acting in place of the famous Cardinal Mindzenty, who had been arrested and detained years before. Based on the so-called evidence, provided by the prisoner, the Foreign Ministry announced that henceforth it would not honor the diplomatic list. As a result of the shrinking of the staff, we were obliged to move from the house where we had had so much fun to a house owned by the Legation. The parties were over.

Bebi decided she had to take bold steps to get out of the country for the sake of her son, Hubert. She divorced her husband, which relieved him of any responsibility for her disappearance, and went on her way to Vienna with Hubert drugged in the trunk of the Turkish ambassador's car. The Turks were not as closely watched as some other people, namely the British and we Americans, so it was worth the chance. Besides, Bebi was beautiful and very charming. She married someone in Vienna in order to get a passport. I never knew the details of that chapter, but she always wanted to go to America and that's where she managed to end up, in Washington, D.C., as the wife of a *Newsweek* correspondent . She became, without a great delay, the most sought-after interior designer in that sophisticated place, especially among the foreign diplomats. It was not a hindrance that she spoke, besides her native tongue, fluent German, French, and English with just enough beguiling accent to add to her personal gifts.

Her sister, Nuni, waited until 1956 when the Hungarians staged an almost perfect uprising. Although it ultimately failed, it did provide a window of opportunity to a lot of people who somehow got themselves to Vienna, where they were transported by the U.S. Air Force to Camp Kilmer in New Jersey. Nuni, also a person of great taste, went right to work. She had a series of jobs in smart shops and waited for "Mr. Right" to come along, which he did. She still lives in the apartment on 68th Street in New York which she bought years ago with her first earnings. Both of those girls knew how to handle money.

Early in our sojourn in Budapest my father died. He was only fifty-six years old and apparently had a bad heart that none of us were aware of. I was not able to go to the memorial service, which from all accounts was a fitting tribute to one of Chicago's favorite sons at the Rockefeller Chapel on the campus of the University of Chicago. Robert Maynard Hutchins, who knew my father well and was acquainted with his many services to the University and to the city, was the speaker. The reason I had to miss it was that the nearest airport from which I could catch a plane to the U.S. was in the Russian zone of Vienna, and to get there in time was just not possible. It was a bitter blow, as

I was especially attached to my father. I mourned, but I discovered the next summer when I went home for my sister's wedding that it started all over again. He wasn't there.

One afternoon the maid announced that there were three nuns downstairs who wanted to see me right away. They had a very long and fat carton which contained something they wanted to show me, so I invited them to open it up. It took several minutes, as it was carefully and thoroughly wrapped, and it was very large. I didn't hold my breath until after I saw that it contained a huge bolt of the most exquisite lace I had ever seen. One of the nuns said, "This is the lace from Princess Zita's coronation veil. We want you to buy it."

I was stunned. I knew that Zita was the last Empress of the Austro-Hungarian Empire and that she had lived at Schoenbrun, a palace outside of Vienna where we had gone sightseeing so many times. I found my breath in a minute and replied that I couldn't possibly afford it, adding that I was sorry.

"Oh, please, you are American," the nun said, looking and sounding desperate. "If you can't buy it all, we can sell part of it. You see, we have very little food at the convent. We know you will help us." When I offered to give her a donation, she seemed offended. So finally I agreed to buy three meters, which, I explained, might be used as part of my sister's wedding veil the following summer.

I shuddered when she took out a pair of scissors. I got the measuring tape, while her colleagues held the bolt. They went away content, but I continued being regretful until I finally saw the lace on my sister's head.

One day, a Hungarian friend, a journalist, asked me to meet her at Gerbeau, a fancy meeting place, for tea. I was

Albert's passport photo, 1946,
en route to being the
Third Secretary in
the legation in Tangier

Abdel Kadir and Halima with
Peter on her back

Our house in
Tangier, 1946

Peter going for a donkey ride in our garden

Howard Elting with Susan in Morocco

Our first house in Budapest, 1949

A porcelain stove in our
Budapest sitting room

This sign appeared one night
on our front gate:
*Buy Peace Bonds and Give
an Answer to the American
Imperialists*

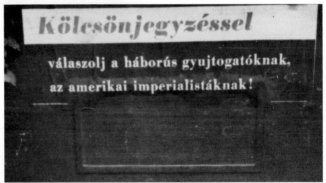

At the border crossing with Austria after being expelled
from Hungary, July 1951

The Prague embassy,
1957

In Prague, 1958, with our English nanny Barbara

Anna Dobrowolska, our housekeeper in Prague, who came to visit us in Michigan in 1973

Our house on Lowicka Street, Warsaw, 1964

A picnic in the woods with the Cabots – not just a chance to eat, but an opportunity to speak freely

The Bialy Słon sale in Warsaw, 1963

Albert and me in the back garden of our rented house
in Joze, France, summer 1962

The whole family in Warsaw, September 1962

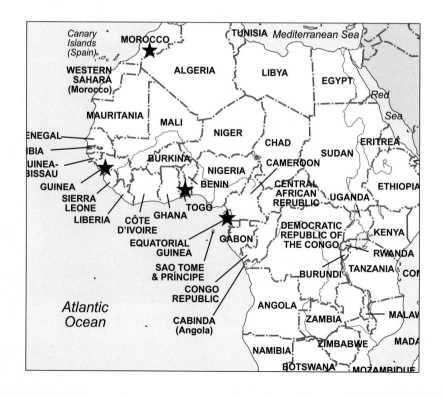

surprised but delighted, as I was an admirer and, of course, my curiosity was piqued. We chatted for a while and finally she said, "Carroll, I have a serious request." My imagination did not stretch far enough to anticipate what she asked. "Will you take the two girls out?"

I was speechless for a long time. I knew I had to say *no*, but I hadn't the heart or the wits to figure out how to do it. She went on, "I think Endre and I will be arrested soon, and I don't know what will happen to them."

Her husband was also a journalist and a very fine one. What she was telling me was undoubtedly the truth. Finally I gave the most direct answer, the most truthful answer there was. "Ilonka, if I did what you are asking, I would jeopardize the entire American mission. I think the AVO (secret police) is waiting for me to do something against the law, something stupid, and Heaven knows I am surrounded by temptations every day." I would have had to smuggle those children somehow in a diplomatic mail pouch or in the trunk of my car. There was no way to keep it secret anyway.

She was sad, but she knew exactly why it was impossible. I wondered later whether the police hadn't put her up to asking. But she was my FRIEND. I was still too naïve to believe it.

Everything happened as she predicted. She and her husband were, indeed, arrested, and the children went to stay with their grandparents. But this story has a happy ending. In 1956 when there was an uprising in Hungary, a few precious days when, rather like the Bastille during the French Revolution, the prisons were opened and hundreds of people escaped, Ilonka and Endre got to Vienna and from there to Camp Kilmer in New Jersey, courtesy of the U.S.

Air Force. Their former employers, the United Press and the Associated Press gave them jobs in Washington and their brilliant daughters went to the best schools and have been creative, successful citizens ever since, the same as in a fairy tale.

Another story, more typical, concerns a small playgroup I organized for my children with one of the few Hungarian families I knew. It came to a shocking and abrupt halt one day when they called breathlessly in the morning and asked me to come to their house right away. I could tell that they really meant right away, immediately, so I did my best. When I arrived, the mother came to meet me at the gate and explained that they had received orders to prepare for departure in twenty-four hours. They would be transported to the Hortobagy, a dry, barren area, and left to start whatever they could make of a new life with whatever they could carry. The order did not include the whole family. Their son had married a chambermaid so she and the children, being people's people, could remain on the place. The grandparents wanted to sell me anything in the house to raise a little cash. Everyone was crying, the children too, and it was hard to think.

Finally I bought a sofa, typical of the style that people favored then in that part of Europe. I still have that sofa. The cushions are filled with real Hungarian goose feathers, and it is everyone's favorite. No one cares where it came from. Only I think about that family every time I make myself comfortable there. The mother asked me to buy a gold watch, a delicate little thing, with an aquamarine for a crystal. When I told her I would try to find another buyer, she thrust it in my hand and said, "No, I want you to have it." Afterwards I was never able to wear it because of the memories it elicited, so I gave it to my brother's fiancée. The story of that family was repeated all over town. The police would pound on the door, almost always at night, I guess for the scare factor. Otherwise why did they do it in such a cruel way? As far as I know, the grandparents never saw the children again.

When both of my children caught whooping cough and were still hacking away after six months, the local pediatrician advised me to rent an airplane and take them for an hour's ride in rare air. I had never heard of that treatment, but I was ready to try almost anything. I settled on a compromise and took them to a mountain retreat above Bad Gastein in Austria. It worked. After only a few days they stopped coughing and color began to return to their poor, drawn faces. My mother came to be with us, and shortly Albert turned up. By that time, he was coughing that typical whooping sound that is no other disease. But he insisted that it could not possibly be whooping cough. He had really come to Bad Gastein to tell me that the Secret Police were on to some Hungarian contact he had which, he presaged, would eventually mean the end of his tenure in Budapest, because some putative information of value had been exchanged. It all had to do with the arrest and trial of Robert Vogeler, an employee of ITT (International Telephone & Telegraph) who came to Budapest shortly before our arrival to work out some sort of business deal with the Hungarian government. Everyone in the Legation thought he was rather a loudmouth, bragging about exploits and near misses with the secret police (AVO). We were sorry but not surprised when he was arrested and not released until April of 1951 after a long public trial.

It was the 5th of July, 1951, the day after our national day party that the diplomatic note arrived giving us twenty-four hours to get out of the country. Due to a rare and bizarre situation in the Legation, I had been the hostess at the party. The Minister was on leave, and the wife of his deputy was in Switzerland because she had had a nervous breakdown. This left me, due to the reduced size of our staff, the ranking lady. So I stood at the head of the receiving line greeting the guests as they arrived. The government people must all have known that by the next day, I would be *persona non grata*, which inhibited them not at all from attending the party, kissing my hand and enjoying my champagne. Later that elevated them in my mind on the scale of rats.

The diplomatic note arrived at about 1 p.m., which was an inconvenient time because Vienna was five hours away, and the question immediately became: which would be the least traumatic for the children – to pack everything we could in the next two hours and head for the border or to pack more leisurely and leave early the next morning. We made the latter choice. We had two personal cars so we could take a significant amount of personal effects and still leave the back seat empty for two small people and their peanut butter sandwiches. If you can imagine, the political air was rotten enough at that time to cause Albert to travel with a loaded .45 on the seat next to him. We had been so vilified on the radio and in the press during and after the trial of the American businessman that we had no idea what the authorities might try at the last minute. The only diplomat who came to see us off was the Dutch Ambassador, which prompted the special soft spot in my heart for the kind of independent, brave and gallant behavior of the Dutch, which I realize now is historic. Special armed sentries had been stationed outside our house, so there was no mistake about who came and went.

About half way to Vienna, a terrible surprise! My station wagon had a flat tire. No lug wrench was to be found since, in our haste to prepare for a speedy departure, we had not had the cars checked for a trip. As we stood in the road pondering a solution with the clock ticking, a Russian truck driven by a Hungarian driver stopped, and the driver asked what he could do to help. In the end, he did everything to help because his truck had an air compressor under the hood, and he used it to get us on our way again. I gave him a carton of American cigarettes, pure gold at the time. He kissed my hand and blessed us all in a typical, chivalrous Hungarian way. I still love him. In the end we arrived at the border with half an hour to spare. While many American diplomats have been summarily expelled from their posts since that time, in 1951 it was shocking.

Vienna, even under those circumstances, was the same kind of treat it had always been, even though it, too, was a wreck. We stayed in the Army's hotel, which was reserved for officers with children. It was called the Cottage Hotel, I think because it was in the elevated part of town and had, before the War, been a tuberculosis sanitarium with that name. But surely there was a better place to recover from TB than "Le Grand Hotel du Cottage" as neighbors we knew later in Washington always called it. If nothing else, it would have been the jars of baby food on every table that might have cured them. We sold one of our cars in Vienna and sailed home slowly on a luxurious liner, just what we needed before settling down to a suburban life in Maryland, the first house we had ever owned and the arrival of a welcome third child named Anthony.

In Washington Albert was immediately swallowed up by

the Office of Eastern European Affairs working mostly on Rumanian problems, whatever they were at the time. I remember particularly the case of the Georgescu family, which had been separated when the father and mother came to the U.S. on Standard Oil business. They wanted to have their two sons follow them, but the Rumanian government would not consider a humanitarian gesture, even of that small proportion. Albert spent part of the next two years helping to resolve that stalemate and similar ones. You can imagine my satisfaction when many years later I saw a handsome gentleman on television named Peter Georgescu, one of the sons, a big shot at Young and Rubicam, the advertising agency.

People wonder, I think, what all those bodies in the State Department on C Street in Washington are doing. The Georgescu story is typical. They are cajoling, they are trading, they are maneuvering. The young ones are turning into seasoned diplomats. That's how it happens. No one who starts at the top - the so-called "political appointees" because they are friends of the President - has the same skills. They don't come naturally, as many people think. Of course education and personality bear on how a solution to a diplomatic problem is arrived at, but nothing equals experience. This can probably be said of every achiever in the world including Donald Trump and George Soros, who have nothing else in common with diplomats.

CHAPTER SEVEN

Intrigues Not to Write Home About

IN 1955 WE WERE ENTHUSIASTIC about an assignment to Prague. Problems for the United States resulting from the necessity and difficulty in dealing with the communist governments of Eastern Europe seemed most urgent then, and we were beginning to know something about them. I felt strangely at home right from the beginning, which I soon realized was from the acrid smell of brown coal, which was the same as Chicago at the time. The city and its environs, disheveled although almost untouched in the Second World War, was a constant treasure chest of historical beauty and mystery. Somehow I managed to gain admittance to a ballet class at the Opera Ballet School. The students were mostly children or young women who needed the exercise like me. The difference was that the others had had considerable training. I tried not to get in their way, and so did Flora Lewis, a reporter for the *Washington Post*, also brave and bold. I think the teacher liked having us there, although we were a lot of trouble because we had to do everything at least twice.

Even though I was never able to make a real friend outside my diplomatic circle, the history to be learned and local color to be appreciated made up somewhat for the isolation. Besides, we had a nice apartment in the Chancery building and I had a good job teaching three teenaged girls using a Calvert curriculum. The young diplomatic crowd was lively and game for any permissible diversion. The Counselor of the British Embassy composed a musical comedy cadging music mostly from Gilbert and Sullivan, which he called "La Vie En Rouge". I helped as much as I could with rhymes and directing. In the end, we presented it to the Western corps in someone's house. It was recorded and made quite a hit with the frustrated diplomats, so I took it to Vienna and had 78 records made, which sold well among the young sector of the diplomatic corps.

One of the several ways the Foreign Ministry used to keep track of foreigners was through the so-called "Office of Services," to whom we were obliged to apply whenever we wished to engage any kind of household help. Since we were very junior in rank we rarely had our choice of personnel with highly developed skills. The first nanny they sent was charming and had good English, but it turned out, after hours she worked as a call girl at the Alcron Hotel, so as soon as she found someone who offered to get her out of the country, she was gone. She confided to me that she was on her way so I lent her my best suitcase, which she said she would leave at the American Embassy in Vienna. Of course, I never saw it again.

I soon discovered, because I occasionally did some substitute teaching at the small International School housed in our Embassy, that Peter, then age nine, was too energetic and innovative to be cooped up in such a limited environment.

Among the experimental high jinks he engaged in to relieve the boredom was putting the braids of the girl sitting in front of him in his ink well. She happened to be the daughter of the Swedish Ambassador, our friend. The best solution we thought of was sending him to boarding school in England where, conventional wisdom to the contrary, he was very happy.

While in London I engaged a professional nanny named Barbara who said she understood that fraternizing with Czechs was not permitted. She liked to knit and do crossword puzzles, she said. The first night Barbara was in Prague, our cook, Anna, a delightful girl about Barbara's age, mid-twenties, who could speak practically no English, asked me if she might take Barbara out to have a look around the city. I could see no harm in that. In fact I thought it was a very friendly gesture, so I agreed. Some time during the evening, the two girls were having a coffee in a café where two young men were seated at the next table. Of course, conversation soon seemed necessary. Both the gentlemen were professional oboe players; both were very "nice". That's all I knew for a while. Often the girls would go out for an evening together, but I never heard anything except that they had enjoyed a concert on occasion. Finally I realized that Barbara sometimes came home with a box of chocolates or a bunch of roses. I knew that the poor simple girl had never had attention like that before.

It wasn't until the summer that it dawned on me that Barbara was pregnant, and she finally admitted to it. We had gone for holiday to a simple little town on the Adriatic coast of Italy where she constantly complained of nausea, diagnosed by the doctor we consulted there as a liver problem.

I insisted that that she go home to have her baby so it could have a British passport, but first she needed to be married. So as soon as we returned to Prague, we had a magnificent ceremony in the famous St.Vitus Cathedral. The bride was dressed in a fluffy gown that I had worn as a bridesmaid, I think, at the wedding of one of my sisters. She carried a bouquet of roses, while Stefan, the other oboist, played Smetana in the loft with organ accompaniment. The music and the sight of our family all dressed up gathered a small crowd which filtered into the cathedral for the ceremony, giving it a true festive feeling. Barbara and Zdenek had a short honeymoon in the countryside somewhere and then she left. I never saw her again. I know only that she returned and traveled around with her husband to small vacation spots run by the Communist Party for workers on holiday. The accommodations were miserable. It was difficult finding necessary food and other provisions for their child, and Barbara never learned to speak Czech well enough to run her daily life, so the inevitable divorce came within a year.

Was it inevitable that Anna repeat all of Barbara's mistakes? I thought not because she had her family in Prague, and they were religious. But I shouldn't have been as surprised and disgusted as I was when she announced that she needed to get married. It was a severe blow to her mother that Anna chose to be married during Lent. We repeated the same scenario that we had devised for Barbara: the Cathedral wedding, a dress from my closet, flowers, and music provided by Barbara's husband. The bride's family had a reception after the wedding, which we did not attend because it was one of the nights Albert was due to sleep in the code room, a necessary duty for all the FSO's living in

the Chancery building because of our very small staff. I
went to dinner that night in the apartment of one of our
colleagues who lived in another courtyard in the same
ancient palace. That night a strange event took place, a
long story.

First I must explain that after Barbara had left, I decided
to give the Sprava Sluzba (Office of Services) another try.
They sent me a jolly young woman with an ample bosom,
which made her seem more approachable and lovable than
her English predecessor. She had excellent English, which
I valued for my youngest child, then only two years old.
She seemed heaven-sent, and nothing that happened
proved otherwise even though I eventually realized that
she must have given the STB (secret police) excellent
reporting on a steady basis.

At about 3 a.m. after Anna's wedding, our dog, sleeping
by my bed, suddenly jumped up and began to bark furious-
ly, a sound I had never heard before. He was ordinarily a
very mild-mannered fellow. There being no entry or exit to
the street we were not accustomed to unscheduled visits. I
lay still in my bed until I heard a knock on the door right
beside me, which faced the central stairway. I leapt up then
and reached for the coat on the floor, which had once been
part of my trousseau and had ended up as a dog bed. I put
it on over my nightgown and opened the door a few inches. A man whom I had not seen before was standing very
close to the door, but he didn't put his hand on it or take
a step forward so I was not as alarmed as I might otherwise
have been. He spoke very rapid Czech, something about
Hungary and something about political asylum.

"Czekaj," I said, "wait." I remembered the old-fashioned
army field telephone which had recently been installed in our

bedroom and which I had not had occasion to use before. I cranked the crank several rounds, which seemed like a lot of cranks, but it worked. Albert came on and I said in my calmest tone, "I have a visitor over here and I would like some company."

Albert must have rung the lines of all our neighbors because almost immediately I had a sleepy air attaché and a ghostly administrative officer, both in their bathrobes, walking up the stairs to our apartment. In the meantime I had ushered my visitor into a small sitting room where he and I both sat staring at each other. I was still dressed in the dog bed. My mental picture of the scene is absolutely clear, which doesn't prevent me from wishing I had a photograph of it. What came as no surprise was that my outside telephone rang and Albert instructed me to ask one of the "bathrobes" in the hall to go to the code room, which was close by in the building, to relieve him so he could deal with the situation at hand himself.

When he arrived, naturally disheveled since he had been sound asleep just a few minutes before, our visitor remained completely calm sitting on the sofa and told us a long tale about being on a train and talking so sympathetically about the Hungarians who had recently failed in a revolution against their communist overlords that he had been arrested and taken off the train at Bydgoszc, where he claimed to have escaped from the police. How he got himself, or said he did, from there to Prague was not clear to me or, I believe, to anyone else in the room. It had been raining all evening but there were no visible signs of weather on his coat or shoes. Albert decided to call in the formidable Joe Jacyno, a Foreign Service Officer, who was of Czech parentage, knew the language thoroughly, had been a colonel in the Marine Corps during the war and was tough. They met in some unused office in the building, sat the fellow down and shone a light in his eyes like Perry Mason. They eventually found out how he got into our supposedly secure building and decided that he was no more than an *agent provocateur* who would, of course, not be granted asylum. They ended up leading him to the spot at the top of the walled garden where he said he had entered and heaving him down into the public park fifteen feet below. Those present at our encounter with the intruder agreed that no word of the event would go beyond our group. It would have been too unsettling for the families who lived in the embassy to think that our putative fortress could be penetrated.

When Albert came home in the morning, he asked me to put down on paper every detail I could remember about the event. So I wrote a little story, which I entitled "The Night Visitor by Amahl," which disappeared into the bowels of the State Department never to be seen again. Years later when I visited the Embassy, I found that the space we had occupied was transformed into Marine quarters, a wry quirk of destiny. We could have used those Marines.

CHAPTER EIGHT
Briefly, A Tame Life

W HEN WE RETURNED TO WASHINGTON, Albert was once again in the Office of Eastern European Affairs where he belonged. We settled down to a relatively quiet life in a comfy house we bought in Chevy Chase D.C. Albert was assigned to the Polish Desk this time which was a lively place, and he was able to make time for a special project which he worked on at home and at the office. Ready reference to the names and offices of high functionaries in Eastern European countries was not available at that time, so he composed a sort of dictionary in chart form that would provide this information handily. When it was finished, he had a chance to publish it commercially, but he declined the offer because he insisted that too much of it had been researched on government time. So it was published by the Government Printing Office, and he was satisfied. Twice in his career he was offered juicy spots on the Paris Embassy staff but he turned them down both times. I was sorry about that, but his excuse both times was, "I don't want to go to all those Red Cross balls."

Susan took easily to the National Cathedral School in Washington. Peter at first didn't seem to fit anywhere. His English accent, his clothes, his vocabulary, and almost everything else simply were not for the sixth grade in the nearby public school so we advanced him to the Alice Deal Junior High, where he finally caught on and did reasonably well. After two years we put him in private school where the social pressures were not so overwhelming and he could be a real star. This was an important development because we knew that in another year we would be moving on and we needed to make some long-range plans for our children.

Tony, now the Headmaster of a school in Denver, was untamable. I tried two or three different kindergartens where he managed to disrupt the class and learn nothing discernable. When I took him to the Beauvoir School in Washington to be tested for entrance into kindergarten, the school responded by telling me that they were unable to accept him because they judged him to have a hearing defect. I asked him what the test was like and he explained that there was a very large teacher sitting on a very small chair "just like mine and I was really afraid she would fall off. She had a piece of paper with some boxes drawn on it and some camels. She kept asking me to tell her which camel was halfway in the box and which one was outside and which one was all the way in and things like that. I thought she couldn't tell so I asked her why not."

Obviously the teacher thought he couldn't hear. I don't blame her. I had his hearing tested immediately afterward with a completely positive report. And so it went. Several years later at the International School in Warsaw he was not permitted to ride the school bus because he persisted in telling stories, despite several requests that he not tell stories to the children because they arrived at school too excited to settle down to their work. He soon found himself walking to school every day with his father, not exactly a punishment for either one of them.

CHAPTER NINE

We All Keep Learning

In 1961 we leapt at a chance to go to Harvard's
Center for International Affairs. We had a good time in
Cambridge partly because it was an interesting place to be
but also because it gave us the opportunity we needed to fit
our two older children into schools where we would be
willing to entrust them when we left to go to Warsaw a year
later. Peter went to Groton as a boarder and Susan went to
Concord Academy as a day student, where she was able to
board the next year when we left. She has told me many
times that she learned everything she knows at Concord. I
guess college at Sarah Lawrence was not as fruitful intellec-
tually or otherwise for her at that time, which coincided
with the years of campus unrest and revolt. Peter was not
particularly happy, but I didn't know what to do about it,
except to return every once in a while to talk to him and
the Headmaster, who always told me Peter was "great."
Now in his middle age he agrees that those school years
and the friends he made there were "great." He wouldn't
miss a reunion.

As anticipated, we went off to Warsaw in the fall of 1961,
Albert as Deputy Chief of Mission (or "Counselor" as the

job is sometimes called). It was a challenging jump in status because when the Ambassador is not in residence, the DCM is "it". One of the reasons that Warsaw was perhaps my favorite post is that Ambassador John Moors Cabot was an experienced old Foreign Service Officer (FSO) whose wife I admired for her taste, her devotion to the cause, her belief in the importance of fun, her toughness, her discretion - all qualities required of diplomats' wives. She was also well aware of her own limitations, not trying to learn Polish as I did, probably because in her job French would do very well. I came to love her as much as anyone I have known. After they had retired and were living in a lovely Georgetown house, she always insisted that we stay there whether they were at home or not. We often visited them in Manchester, MA, the place nearest and dearest to their hearts. Now that it is over, I realize that one easy way a person can guarantee being remembered is to give small presents. Elizabeth gave me small presents often, usually for no particular reason, a scarf or an unusual handbag. I think of her every day twenty-five years later. It was sad but flattering that when Elizabeth was dying, she wanted to see me. I took along some good photographs I had of our husbands together and great ones of Sunday picnics in the woods outside of Warsaw, where the Cabots would lay out oriental rugs and our pot luck menu always included a bit of Zubrowka, Poland's finest vodka.

We felt we could talk about anything out there without being overheard, but I always had my doubts. If the opposition was interested in us for any reason, there was no place to hide. Security people from the State Department came out once or twice a year to scan our private quarters for listening devices which, if not replaced *in situ* were probably replaced in a new location. One year they took up the floorboards under the coffee table in our living room and found an old-fashioned tape recorder spinning around which was traced to the house next door with which we shared a common wall. For all we knew, it was reactivated the next day but we didn't care. If we wanted to discuss sensitive issues we could go to the Embassy where there was a "secure room". We simply became a little more vigilant. That's all we could do.

Albert and I did discover one place, which felt very private, where we never went with anyone else. It was also within half an hour of the city limits, a place where there were two small ponds devoted to raising frogs to ship to France where the superior quality of the meat on their legs was most appreciated. The fisherman sat on the edge of the pond holding a long bamboo cane, about eight feet long, with a three-inch square of bright red cotton cloth at the end which he slapped gently up and down on the surface of the water. Like many Polish innocents at the time, the frogs gathered around the color red where the fishermen could pick them up with a net. Each frog would be judged for weight and general plumpness by the old fisherman, who had obviously judged thousands of frogs over the years. If the frog in hand was thought to weigh less than ten *decas*, he was tossed back into the pond to fatten up and be harvested another day.

Our children came home (Warsaw, for the time being) for holidays, Christmas and Easter. In the summer of 1962 through the good offices of Mme. D'Arcy, the French teacher at Concord Academy where Susan was a student, I was able to rent a typical French family summer house in a village called Joze near Vichy. Without this connection I would not have succeeded in arranging this splendid opportunity. Everything in France is complicated and, much as I hate to say so, everyone is a snob. The house belonged to a priest who employed as caretaker a Mme. Constant, who tended a small sort of 7/11 shop situated on the other side of the wall that surrounded our house. She was not a character in a Dickens novel, but she could have been. I had to work hard to gain her favor. It was conservative rural France and therefore more complicated than Paris. At my request she sent me a woman who could cook our dinners. This woman was called "Felicie," a misnomer if there ever was one, but she made good hollandaise sauce and it was artichoke season. We gradually gained mutual confidence, although the poor soul never learned the value or power of a smile.

The house was perfect for us. I imagined that for several generations our host family had stored there the furniture they were replacing in their city digs. Nothing matched anything else. It was a fascinating study in styles and colors. There were gilt tables mixed with odd country pieces and dilapidated comfortable chairs of various style. We had no refrigerator, but learned quickly the value of a cold cellar dug into the side of a hill on the property, as well as the reason for food shopping on a daily basis. We sent Tony twice daily to the baker to buy fresh bread. He soon became known in the village as "le petit bonhomme du pain". We made excursions every day, a picnic lunch somewhere in the countryside, and since we were in the heartland of Romanesque architecture, we visited the famous churches always with "Guide Bleu" in hand. When we felt like having a breath of city air we went to Clermont-Ferrand where I could emote over the gorgeous equestrian statue of

Vercingétorix in the main square. We had important errands in the city as well. Peter was dieting and exercising vigorously in an effort to lose a considerable amount of poundage he had acquired at school. We went to town once a week solely for the purpose of having him put a few francs into a public scale, which progressively over the weeks demonstrated that he was definitely on the right track. As a result we needed to shop for new clothes once in a while, a great diversion for all of us. By the end of the summer he was extremely chic.

One day, arriving home from just such an excursion, we found a dromedary reclined in our front yard, a member of a gypsy circus which was pitching its tent in the schoolyard across the street. Not wanting to give Mme. Constant any excuse for complaint about our stewardship of the property, I went over and asked the person I identified as the boss to remove the dromedary. "But," he explained in broken French, "we always leave her there." And so I learned that the circus was an annual event and, contrary to what I would have expected, the villagers tolerated it. I didn't want to argue with the boss anyway. So the dromedary stayed except, of course, when it was performing in the tent. The tent was round, and maybe could hold two hundred people, but there were not that many the night we went. There were trapeze artists and a tired lion, who was, nevertheless, scary because we were so close. The unforgettable act, however, was that provided by a desultory wild boar tied by a piece of flimsy rope. We knew something about wild boars because their meat is greatly prized in Poland and we had a cook who was a genius boar-cooker. We served it as often as we could get it. The circus boar looked small, dirty, and harmless. He had curly tusks, perhaps his tools for digging truffles.

However, when the ringmaster challenged the audience to ride the boar, no one responded. I could feel the vibes from Tony seated next to me. "Mom. Should I go?" I wanted to say yes but I lost my nerve. I still feel guilty because it would have been the experience of a lifetime. And a little boy, a member of the circus family, who obviously had done it dozens of times, jumped on the boar's back and raced at top speed round and round the ring.

Over the intervening years, I had kept in contact with Ruth and Ian Bell, English diplomats whom we had known in Prague. It was Ian who had authored "La Vie en Rouge" which provided a necessary outlet and many jolly times for all the junior diplomats. During the time we were posted in Warsaw, they were in Lyon, and it suddenly occurred to me that since we were reasonably close, it would be a good idea to impose on their friendship and take the children south to see the Avignon region, the Pope's palace and the Roman ruins still standing in so many locations there. I telephoned the Bells (from the post office since we had no private phone) and it was soon arranged that I would drive to Lyon with all three children, leave Tony with the Bells (whose son was his age) and continue on with the older ones. I have no idea what they recall of this escapade, but I remember well and with much pleasure the aquaducts, the palaces, the countryside, the food. I still believe, as many people do, that Lyon and environs is the gustatory capitol of the western world, a theory we put to the test one night. On our way back to the Bells we ran into an indescribable downpour, which we had to traverse on the way to their house. Just on the outskirts of the city, the electricity failed, and we had only our car lights to guide us. I stopped at two or three restaurants to beg for dinner. I didn't need to try to look pitiful. I WAS pitiful. Even my shoes were full of water and my clothes and hair were skin tight. We did finally find a place where the door was opened and my plea was taken under consideration seriously enough to elicit the following judgment, "Oh, you wouldn't be able to pay. This is a very fine restaurant."

So I was obliged to appeal to French snobbery, which I knew was there. "Please", said I, "We are on our way to the British Consul General. Let us change our clothes somewhere. We will get our suitcases which are in our Mercedes right here."

Well, it worked, ashamed as I am for revealing my use of a technique I despised. We were shown to the waitresses' dressing room with a single candle. We even managed to arrange our hair well enough to satisfy our hostess and were shown to a table. It was fascinating how in a very few minutes a "coq au vin," along with accompanying vegetables, was pulled out of a kettle in front of our eyes, still in its string bag, and deftly distributed, the juiciest parts, onto our three plates. Do we have reasons to remember that meal?

Inevitably the time came for all of us to pack up and go back to our jobs. The two children in eastern schools in the States always traveled together from Warsaw to Boston. The State Department paid for these trips as long as we used American carriers, namely Pan American. We had done it so many times there were no histrionics. We were all growing up grieving on the inside, stalwart on the outside, essential to our survival in the long run.

In order to raise money to pay for a splendid Christmas party that the American staff of the embassy gave for the Polish employees and their families each year, the embassy wives put on a giant sale, which we called "Bialy Slon" (literal translation "White Elephant"). We collected anything that people departing the post decided they no longer needed to haul around the world, which could be anything from bicycles to outgrown clothing to radios and American television sets. The sorting and the pricing were a tremendous amount of work, but well worth it because it was a bonding project for the American staff and a much-appreciated event for all the buyers. Somewhere, deep down, every little girl likes to play "store." Many amusing stories are to be told about those sales. For instance, when the Ambassador's wife donated one of her husband's coats to the sale (which he very much regretted), she insisted that he attend the sale as the doors opened in order to buy his coat back. Another more interesting recollection is the sight of three perfect little Tyrolean coats left over at the end of one of our sales which no Pole wanted to buy because they were German, not a popular look for children or anyone else in those days, no matter how severe the winter.

Looking back, the most onerous task I had to perform in Poland was escorting visitors to Auschwitz. Every Congressman who came around needed to say he had seen it. When I first went there in 1961, the grounds were still in the condition they had been when the liberation took place, except that scrubby grass and weeds had grown up everywhere, which only added to the desolate spookiness of the place. The ovens, two of them inside just to the left of the famous archway proclaiming "Arbeit Macht Frei" still smelled of smoke. That memory will never leave me. What happened later was somehow even worse. The entire area was gradually beautified - flower beds along manicured walkways, exhibitions of eyeglasses taken from inmates before they went to be gassed, collections of shoes, such as they were, and gold from teeth were all arranged in showcases. Even though the effect was tamer by far than when I had originally seen it, when I took my mother there at her request she refused to get out of the car.

Visiting painters and sculptors in their studios and assembling a collection of unique and wondrous pieces of art, which I live with to this day, was my most satisfying form of recreation. Artists' supplies were very scarce at that time, so much ingenuity was required to produce an effect that would satisfy the creator. I have a large watercolor painted on graph paper. I have a fascinating still life painted on a 24x19-inch piece of particleboard with a frame painted right into the picture. When Katherine Kuh, the famous curator and author, was engaged by the First National Bank to assemble a worthy collection for the main bank in Chicago and a few of their overseas branches, she included Warsaw in her list of important targets. Being an old friend, she got in touch with me as soon as she hit the ground and allowed me to introduce her to some of my favorites. I tell you, that was fun! She must have had an unlimited budget. She also had a super eye for skill and originality, so I gained a lot just sitting and listening to her talk. We were both amazed that I had learned a useful amount of Polish to be a translator of sorts. She visited and searched many European cities which she knew to be producing innovative work. The collection became so valuable that later it was withdrawn from foreign sites and brought back to what was believed to be safer surroundings. That was before we in America saw a terrorist behind every fallen leaf.

These were the glorious years of Kennedy's effort to reach out, to breach the iron curtain which divided us from

Eastern European countries by sending a large number of well-known American artists to perform or lecture or just to meet their counterparts in the eastern bloc countries. All of that was a tremendous joy and source of information for everyone, for students, professors, and ordinary citizens who flocked to hear them and see them. At the time of Kennedy's assassination, we had John Steinbeck, with his very pleasant wife, and a young Edward Albee in town. They, like the general public in Warsaw, were stricken by the news.

A lot has been written about the extraordinary outpouring of admiration and affection demonstrated by the Poles at that shocking time, but being there and feeling it firsthand was an experience quite aside from the fact that we in America had lost an icon. The lobby of the embassy, a handsome new building at that time, was so crowded with visitors, ordinary people waiting to sign the condolence book, that twice during the weeks that followed an ambulance had to be summoned to tend to someone who had been overcome by emotion. There was much weeping and gnashing of teeth. I finally understood what that biblical expression meant. Embassies all over the world were ordered to observe deep mourning for a month when we all wore black and regretted social events. I did invite Albee for lunch one day thinking he would enjoy a meal out of his hotel. He was too upset to enjoy anything, but our children won't forget meeting him and having a chance to ask questions. His most recent work, as I recall, had been *Who's Afraid of Virginia Woolf.* When Peter asked, "Where do you get characters like George and Martha?" he replied, "Oh, I know a lot of people like that." These days I know a lot of people like that myself.

It is not a myth that the Poles are special people. They have as a nation a personality which is unique in Eastern Europe. This came up on a talk show I listened to on National Public Radio recently. Among other things, they talked about the unfortunate words spoken by President Ford when he was running for election in 1976, and he denied that the Poles were under the thumb of the Soviet Union. He was referring to their hearts and minds. The truth is that during those dark days when they lived as pawns of the Soviet Union because the opening for their escape had not yet arrived, the people as well as their puppet government took every opportunity that came along to help us. For instance, one morning in 1966 at about 2 a.m. the telephone rang in our bedroom. It was a friend in the State Department asking Albert to arrange immediately for the arrival of a special plane bringing Averell Harriman to Warsaw to ask the Polish government to intervene with the North Vietnamese on our behalf to start negotiations to end the Vietnam War. We were unaware of the purpose of the visit because it could not be discussed on the telephone. Albert knew only that maximum haste was needed. Harriman's plane at that moment was over Copenhagen, which was little more than an hour away, so there was not much time to arrange landing rights. Among details that Albert needed to know were the identifying numbers of the plane and the passports of everyone arriving on it. Harriman was traveling alone, no secretaries or assistants around while the talks were going on. Albert called the fellow in the Foreign Ministry whom he trusted to act in confidence and quickly to arrange the landing and for an embassy car to meet the plane on the field, usually a drawn-out procedure. These are things a person learns only by experience. That visit did not have the positive result desired, but it at least let the North know that the U.S. was actively seeking an end to the whole miserable story.

I think about pickle soup and succulent wild boar and mushrooms when I think about Poland, but the painters and the composers and the theater and the knowledge that the West was slowly inching up on a long-sought political victory were what made Warsaw an outstanding experience for the whole family of people who served there at that time; but the best, at least for us, was still to come.

CHAPTER TEN

Two Years of Peregrinations

It started with a short tour in the Inspection Corps, that branch of the State Department in charge of making sure that the overseas posts are functioning at top efficiency. To perform this service, teams of inspectors are made up of a high-ranking officer, usually an ambassador, an administrative officer, and a secretary. Albert was assigned to lead one of two teams heading for Mexico where, at that time, the U.S. had sixteen consulates scattered around the country in addition to an enormous embassy in Mexico City. Albert was assigned to half of the consulates and half of the Embassy. It was summer and I needed to stay with the rest of my family in Michigan. So I sent Susan who was in the middle of a typical teenaged "summer of discontent" to keep him company. I think going somewhere helped a little to bring her back to her sense of herself. Maybe that's why she went with him the next summer to West Africa, where she worked for a while with the Peace Corps in a leper colony. I can't imagine what that was like, but it did her no harm. After that, they went on to the Republic of Guinea, where they stayed in an embassy apartment, and she did the shopping and cooking for the inspection team. I don't think she had ever cooked anything before, and certainly she had not obtained the ingredients from an open-air market where most of the wares for sale were unfamiliar. Who knows whether that long-forgotten test kitchen played a part in building the remarkable skill she demonstrates in culinary art today. But I hold to my theory that no experience, although unappreciated at the time, is wasted.

During the winter that intervened between those two summers, we did Vienna and Belgrade. Those were relatively big embassies so the inspection was lengthy, meaning more fun and adventure for me and a lot of learning. There were people at both posts whom I had known before, which is what happens in the Foreign Service and is a great help. After a while you realize that you have a comforting network, even though you are floating around.

CHAPTER ELEVEN

The Best is Yet to Come

In 1968 the first ambassadorial appointment finally came. We were assigned to the Republic of Togo on the West Coast of Africa where most African-Americans trace their ancestry. When Albert appeared before the Senate Foreign Relations Committee for confirmation, Senator Fulbright asked a pertinent question: "Everybody knows you're an Eastern European specialist, so why are they sending you to Africa?"

Albert answered, "I don't know. You'll have to ask the President."

I had already declared that I was tired of the dusty little towns in Eastern Europe and those carbolic acid hotels, and I hoped for a real change. So I didn't care what the answer to the senator's question really was, but I found out later. An old friend of the Democratic Party let it be known to the White House that he would like an ambassadorial post. The only one open at the time, which was considered appropriate for a political appointee, was Dakar, the capital of Senegal. So Rob McIlvaine, a career Foreign Service Officer who was slated to go there, was shifted to the Republic of Guinea and Albert Sherer who was slated for

Guinea was shifted to the Republic of Togo. That's how it works, for better or worse. It turned out, however, that the East-West battle was being fought in Africa as well as in Europe; that is, the battle for hearts and minds.

I left for Togo with the same curiosity and anticipation that I had had twenty-two years before when we went to Tangier. Only this time I thought I knew what I was doing. Lyndon Johnson was President then, and I was delighted when Mrs. Johnson invited me along with wives of newly appointed ambassadors for coffee at the White House. Katie Loucheim, her social secretary, picked me up along with three other women, none of whom I knew, in a long limo which took us right to a White House entrance without stopping to be identified. We were ushered into the private quarters upstairs where Lady Bird was waiting for us, a nice touch, and conversation came easily.

Just as I thought we should be leaving, Marvin Watson appeared at the doorway and said, "Ladies, the President would like to meet you." There was no trumpet announcing his entry, but there didn't need to be. He seemed to fill up the whole room. I don't think he shook our hands, he just sat down, plunk, on the sofa next to me and told us how tired he was of having teachers and preachers tell him how to run the war in Vietnam. We all believed him, partly because he looked so tired and gray and anyway, he was the President of the United States, and we wanted to believe him. He put his hand on my knee during this part of the soliloquy but it was as though he just wanted a place to put it down. So I froze. It was the least I could do for the war effort.

Pan American Airways had two flights a week to the part of the world where we were trying to go, one arriving in

Accra, Ghana, and the other in Cotonou, Benin, neighboring countries to Togo. I couldn't count the number of trips I made to those two places over the next couple of years. Arrival times were *ad hoc* affairs, but I could never figure out why. One of the kids finally commented, "PanAm makes the going stop!" That's the way it seemed. The plane we took for our initial trip, however, was on time and made a special stop in Lomé, where we found the entire array of resident ambassadors and their wives waiting to greet us as well as the staff of our own embassy. I was surprised and puzzled. I soon discovered that the post was so small and sleepy that the arrival of a new American ambassador was an "event". And it was surely an "event" for me. I stepped out of the plane and when I took a deep breath, preparatory to walking down the steps, I thought my trachea must have been permanently damaged. It was 104 degrees hot, nothing like Poland. But I kept smiling. "Si vous ne connaissez pas le Togo, vous ne connaissez pas le monde" (If you don't know Togo, you don't know the world"), a current travel poster proclaimed.

I could see almost right away that I would have truly nothing to do, relatively few formal duties. The house was clean and nicely decorated and well staffed. So I set out to try to know the Togo, that was "the world" by accompanying Albert on his trips up-country to visit Peace Corps volunteers and meet the local governors. It was these trips that opened up an array of possibilities that changed my life. I noticed in the markets and at sites where the colonials had established schools and workshops that there were beautiful and unusual pieces of art and craftsmanship that could perhaps be commercialized. But who had the know-how to staff such an ambitious project to say nothing of the staying power to see it through? It soon became evident that there were other embassy wives longing for a project and some of them, it turned out, thought my idea was worth a chance and were even willing to lend the project some start-up money. I let the idea simmer for a while and continued to travel up-country whenever a chance presented itself.

Soon I had my first up-country exposure, the seed of understanding the big picture. We left our house in Lomé at 7 a.m. accompanied by Mr. Jondoh, a senior Togolese employee of the American Embassy in the political section, and our driver, Paul. We used a Volkswagon truck which had a front and a back seat and plenty of room for baggage, a modern-day covered wagon with a canvas cover in back to keep out the laterite dust. It was an excellent choice, not only because the vehicle is high and heavy, which makes it reasonably comfortable on bad roads, but also because by the time we got home again we had picked up innumerable gifts from village chiefs including a sheep, two chickens and five guinea hens, all alive. Several goats would be delivered to us later. At first I was embarrassed by this unnecessary largesse, but I had to get over it.

The paved road ended even before one reached the city limits of Lomé. The hot season was starting so the roads were dry, but as there were not many other cars, the dust was not as choking as it would be in some other places. The ants were busy building their towers of laterite dust very high to beat the rainy season, which would start in a couple of months. I guess the dust was stuck together with ant spit, which must be a very strong product because the ants made edifices which are sometimes twelve feet tall.

Our first stop was at a village called Keve, where we

were met by the entire village and their chief as well as Mr. Joachim Akouvi, a functionary of the central government known as a Chef de Poste. With great ceremony the Ambassador was asked to review the guard of honor (two soldiers). We visited a small school where there were two Peace Corps Volunteers (PCV), which had been enlarged that year by means of funds provided by the Council on Foreign Relations of Oak Park, Illinois. As I understood it, a Peace Corps Volunteer who was assigned to the school the year before interested the Oak Park people in this project. The money they provided was more than enough to finish the school, so the village embarked on the construction of a library. They were able to provide the walls, but there was no roof, no window frames or doors, and of course no books. They very much hoped we would do something about that.

After the school visit we were taken to the "palaver hut" for speeches and refreshments. We discovered that such a hut exists in every village. It is where the people gather for the equivalent of town meetings and a variety of ceremonies and dances. This particular hut was fancy, had a cement floor, was round and, of course, open at the sides. We sat in great big overstuffed chairs, obligatory for honored guests. I sat next to the chief. When I asked him how it happened that he spoke English so well, he explained that he had learned it in Ghana and had then gone into the Navy (I supposed he meant the British Navy). Later I found out that when the royal family of the village decided to select him as their chief, he was obligated by custom to return to assume his duties whether he wanted to or not. The chieftainship is inherited in the same family, but apparently not always in direct line; in other words, a nephew or cousin or grandson of the deceased chief may succeed him in special cases.

The speeches were not unlike many that we heard later on. The people were grateful to the United States for the aid they received. What was astounding was how little could be made to go a long way in this part of the world. But they are always hoping for more; for example the people in this village were desperately in need of water - clean water. There was a most dreaded disease called "le ver de Guinée" (a kind of filariasis) which came from drinking fresh water from streams and was prevalent in many places. The eggs of the worms hatch out in the blood stream and produce a painful debilitating condition. Well water is free of these beasts, but wells and pumps are expensive and they are easily contaminated.

The Ambassador replied that so far the AID budget had not been announced (refraining from telling them that the Congress is contemplating big cuts), but he was interested in hearing about their problems and when the time came he would do his best. What else could he say?

From Keve we drove just three kilometers to Assahoun where we were received by another big delegation. There we had a self-help market construction project. (We provided a portion of the funds, and the villagers provided the design and the labor.) The market was only half finished, and the speeches we heard there indicated that funds to complete the work were what they were hoping for. We met the market committee, a group chosen to settle any problems the merchants and customers of the market might have in a democratic way. As practically all the merchants in Togolese markets were women they were well represented on the committee. Since we were by that time already somewhat behind on our schedule, we tried politely to decline their offer of refreshments (including, as everywhere, champagne!), whereupon it was decided to give us a huge basket of fresh pineapples and a goat. Needless to say, we were not able to take the goat with us because we still had six days of travel ahead. Undaunted, they agreed to send it to us! In the same village, Assahoun, we visited a weaving atelier which was being enlarged with our self-help funds. They were making unattractive woven tapestries and scarves, but I thought they could eventually channel their talents into something useful commercially.

The whole trip was one big "happening" as far as I was concerned. Even though I had the schedule on a neat typewritten paper in front of me, and even though I had Mr. Jondoh and the driver, Paul, to tell me where we were going next and what would happen there, it always turned out to be a surprise.

We were driving down the road when, suddenly, we were hailed by a car with a Togolese flag on it. It was the Chef de Circonscription of Palimé, our next stop. He joined us in our car, telling his driver to follow along behind, and we proceeded down a road lined on both sides with teak forests to visit the German experimental farm at Avetonou. Here they were raising colossal pigs, a breed called "Large White", on peanuts, manioc and other food found in the region. They had imported some gorgeous cows and a bull from Germany, which they planned to cross with the local breed, which was giving no milk but was fairly resistant to the tsetse fly. The German cows already gave less milk than they did at home, but the Director told us that the yield had leveled off, and although the quantity was less, it was still a great deal more than the Togolese cows had been able to produce, no matter how they were cared for. The Chef Cir thought all the animals were sick, especially the pigs, because they were penned up and many of them were sleeping. The custom there was to let the animals run free all over the village, foraging for food. As a result, they were very alert, but at the same time, very small, skinny and tough. We saw beautiful chickens laying beautiful eggs because they were in cages. They were fed on local produce, and the eggs were becoming progressively cheaper. The farm was only two years old, so they had not started much of an education program yet, but in the long run that was their goal.

Togo was the only country I knew about where the Germans were not only admired but genuinely loved. Everywhere we went we heard allusions to the glorious "temps des Allemands". I gather that they did a lot of building and organized the citizens in the manner that only the Germans know, and they accomplished much more than just putting an indelible cultural seal on the people, which is what the French are famous for. The Germans were aware of all this and, enjoying their popularity, they were doing a great deal of important work in that little country; for example, they built the beautiful new port at Lomé, which could eventually change the economics of the entire region.

Finally we arrived at the town of Palimé. By then we could see big hills all around us, called mountains by the local inhabitants, the highest being 1020 meters. It was cooler and the air much dryer than in Lomé. We drove beyond the town and higher into the hills to the so-called "campement" where we were to spend the night. It was in a heavenly setting, surrounded by teak trees with their enormous flat, dark green leaves, which tinkled as they touched each other in the evening breeze. There were a dozen varieties of mimosa, of course mangoes everywhere, and plenty of birds (which we had missed down on the coast).

We unloaded our suitcases, some good French water, some booze, and the flowers that had been presented to us along the way all morning. I arranged these in a large vase on the lunch table, and we had a good meal there on the terrace, a fine talk with the Chef Cir, and everyone was in a good mood. After lunch the Chef took us first up a very steep, circuitous narrow road, quite overgrown and thoroughly mysterious. At the top, lo and behold, commanding a superb view in every direction of the valleys was a real French chateau. He called the guard to bring the key so that we could look all around inside. It was furnished in a modern style with a few old pieces thrown in and ready to be moved into at any time. It was built by a Frenchman who was living in Lomé and who wanted to sell it because water was at such a premium up there. It was, in fact, unavailable. Apparently he failed to research that point.

From the chateau we went to the Chef Cir's residence for another of what turned out to be a never-ending series of refreshments. This custom had a logical foundation, as most local customs do. A person simply had to sit down and drink something every hour or two in order to avoid dehydration.

That afternoon we visited an agricultural college which would soon open at Tove for students from Togo and neighboring countries. The physical plant was impressive, especially for the architecture. I didn't find out who the architects were, but I noticed that they were doing very interesting and beautiful things especially adapted to Togo's climate—fancy ways of letting in air but not light. This was a French project.

From Tove we continued on to Agou-Gare, where we visited a school built with U.S. self-help funds and with the help of Operation Crossroads, an organization which provided the labor of high school kids during the summer. I saw a little brown plaque in the school which said "Operation Carrefour de Canada, Amerique, et Grand Bretagne". There was a Peace Corps volunteer teaching at the school but we did not meet him.

We reached our rooms at the campement tired and dusty after dark, which meant after six. (There on the equator we had twelve hours of light and twelve hours of darkness all year round.) We said goodnight to both Mr. Jondoh and to Paul as they had relatives in Palimé whom they wanted to see. Our hope of having a quiet evening and early bed was not to be realized, we discovered, when we found the Chef Cir Adjoint (assistant Chef de Circonscription) waiting for us on the terrace of the campement when we came out to have dinner. There had been a misunderstanding between him and his boss with whom I gather he did not get along at all, and he had been unable to pay us some sort of attention or honor that he would have liked to pay and he was there to apologize. He was a very nice young man and wanted very much to talk, so naturally we invited him to stay and eat with us. He wanted to get a scholarship to study somewhere and he wanted to tell us all about his troubles with his boss, so we had a lively and very interesting time; that is, until the boss showed up. The boss could be a politician anywhere. He even had the classical shape for it and loved talking on any subject at all, as long as he had an audience.

The next morning, we left the campement with Paul and Mr. Jondoh at 7:30 a.m. to visit a small ceramics atelier I had heard about the previous day. Ten minutes down the road our truck had a flat tire, not at all a painful event for either of us but a lot of work for Paul and a delay in our schedule. The site of the delay was too romantic to go undescribed. It was on a mountain road, no vehicles at all except ours; occasionally an African woman walked by with a load of coffee or cocoa beans in a huge basket on her head. There was a small silver waterfall cascading down right beside us, but otherwise not a sound to be heard except birdcalls and the tingling of the teaks. It was magic.

The ceramics atelier was a find. I had to convince M. Morin, the director, to hire a large number of apprentices so that they could turn out things in great enough quantity and cheap enough for sale. He was a retired French school teacher, charming and worldly, who had spent all his time since the Second World War in Togo. Art had always been a hobby with him, until the French government gave him a grant to build his house and workshop. He had a half-dozen African artists working there with the local clay. They were turning out some copies of traditional African art, all bad, and some useful items such as plates and casseroles and ashtrays.

While waiting for the tire to be patched (who would dare go up the mountain without a spare?) we visited the marketplace in Palimé with Mr. Jondoh who helped us identify mysterious-looking objects such as round balls of coarse brown African soap, white chalky sticks which are ground up and added to soup (perhaps as in Mexico this explains why everyone has perfect, white teeth), ground manioc and yams which are used to make the national dish known as "fou-fou". I wondered if I would ever learn to eat fou-fou with pleasure. My first impression was that it tasted like library paste with hot sauce.

At 10:00 we left Palimé accompanied by the Deputy Chef Cir and two hours later, after a ride that defied description because of the condition or lack thereof of the so-called roads, we arrived at a little village called Danyi-Apeyeme, where we were met by all the elders of the village (I would willingly wager that between them they were modeling every kind of hat any of us had ever seen) and two PCV's who were working there. The villagers were preparing lunch for us, so after depositing our bags at the Benedictine monastery where we ultimately spent the night, we repaired to the house of one of the volunteers, a two-room affair which the young man had decorated with whatever he had been able to find: enormous snake skins, ceremonial hats, and of course his standard Peace Corps library (each one of them was given a portable collection of one hundred paperbacks which included reference materials, books on the history and natural phenomena of the region, a first-aid guide, and a well-rounded collection of classics and modern fiction).

The village midwife was in the kitchen working on the lunch and when it was ready she came and joined us with some of the elders and the other PCV at the table, which almost filled up the bed-sitting room. We had rice and hot spicy lamb stew, very good, and the most popular beverage, beer from the German brewery in Lomé. When Albert asked John Burns, our host who was doing agricultural work, what kind of rice it was, he replied, "Uncle Ben's. It only costs ten francs more in the shop up here than the local product." We couldn't figure out why. I must add that the midwife was a lovely looking young woman, educated in France, who had a fine sense of humor. (The medical hierarchy in Togo was quite different from anything we were used to. A midwife was a highly skilled person, far outranking a nurse, or a clinical technician, or a "matrone" who was a sort of nurse's aide specializing in maternity cases.)

In this village, unlike any other we visited, there was a Queen, a woman who had been chosen by the other women, to head up their affairs. She was not married to the Chief, but she was important enough in the village to have been in attendance at the meeting at the Chief's house which took place after lunch when a spokesman for the elders delivered a speech to the Ambassador thanking the United States for its aid and especially for the services of John whom they obviously all admired. They needed water more than anything else, but the list of what they needed would fill a book so I won't go any further with that. Because of the lack of AID money, the Ambassador had to reply again that he could make no promises.

After the meeting, John took us to a place where he was trying to get the villagers to help him plant a citrus orchard. They had cleared the land and he was going to show them how to terrace the hill with pineapples so the soil wouldn't disappear during the rainy season. Finally, he hoped to convince them that they should not rely entirely on coffee, which had had some bad years when they all starved. It struck me as odd that a twenty-two-year-old boy from Pittsburgh, Pennsylvania, had to come all that distance to teach the locals something they should have figured out by themselves after all their experiences. It was the only thing that depressed me about the trip – the fact that everywhere the European had put down a stake, the land was blooming and productive, and everywhere else it wasn't.

From John's project, we all went to the high school of the region where the other PCV, Jane Ginsburg, is teaching English. The pupils were mixed ages but looked mostly around sixteen years old. When Jane asked the Ambassador if he had any questions for the class he asked them to tell him what state in the United States their teacher is from. They knew the answer to that right away so Albert said, "Turn-about is fair play. Who has a question for *me?*"

After a few seconds of embarrassed silence, a hand went up in the back of the room and a boy asked, "Can you tell us why the United States is fighting in Vietnam?"

Well! Ahem! Albert talked very slowly and simply about how much we value the right of free assembly, free speech, free press, and so forth which they understood perfectly and then explained that we were trying to defend all those things in South Vietnam where they are being threatened. Everyone seemed thoroughly satisfied with the answer, and when he asked if there were more questions, a dozen hands shot up. The next question was, "Can you explain to us the list of an ambassador?" After determining that the student meant "role" (having confused it with the morning attendance sheet) Albert was happily answering his inquiry and having a marvelous time when the big fat politician, Chef Cir, walked in, having driven up all the way from Palimé. Not being able to stand the sight of an audience rapt by anyone other than himself, he jumped into the spotlight and spoiled the mood. At any rate, we had seen that they were learning a lot of English, and they had seen that the American Ambassador was a nice fellow, so something was accomplished.

The rest of the afternoon was spent at a convent where some of our self-help funds had been used the year before to repair a roof that was blown off in a cyclone. The sisters there were doing a magnificent job educating girls of all ages in the arts and crafts of becoming homemakers and mothers. This, of course, included a good deal of gardening and poultry raising, as these are traditionally the work of the women (I hadn't quite figured out what the men did). They were teaching the girls how to read and write a little bit and how to sew and how to keep clean. I was very impressed. There was no place to start but at the beginning. There we ran into one of our few friends in the whole of Togo, beautiful Mme. Berger whose husband ran the phosphate mine. She was arranging to rent the convent for the summer as a summer camp for children from the mine families. The climate was much less rigorous up there on what is referred to as "the plateau", much cooler and less humid than in Lomé.

Neither of us ever forgot the night we spent in the Benedictine monastery. There were fifteen monks there, black and white, engaged in agricultural experiments. They had tried growing almonds and olives and figs and a whole lot of crops that had failed. Most of their experiments succeeded, and they were training forty young men a year in the methods they had discovered to be best adapted to the conditions of that region. Their coffee was beautiful because they pruned it right (John was trying to convince his villagers to do this with only limited success). They kept a few African cows (the non-milk-giving sort) in order to have some fertilizer. Their pineapples, papayas, millet, and manioc were the most prosperous we saw anywhere. Their buildings - a main building, a chapel, their living quarters, and a dining hall - were made of the local stone and were very handsome. As part of their tradition, they made their own wine and wonderful jellies from papaya, citrus fruits, and pineapple. As we were being conducted to the dining room by the Father Superior, he mentioned that the monks have a little custom of observing silence during meals and that someone always reads aloud for their edification. That turned out to be literally true, and there was Albert seated next to the beautiful Mme. Berger unable to exchange one single idea with her except by sign language. All the time the monks in turn were reading aloud from first a book (title unannounced) and then from a periodical. The subjects were secular and of some interest to us all, but naturally Albert would rather have talked to Mme. Berger.

Our tour around the grounds and projects of the monks began at 7:30 a.m. When it was completed, we started down the mountain toward Apayeme, John and Jane's village, thinking we would just say goodbye and leave them a bottle of scotch, but when we got there we perceived all the dignitaries of the village outside in the square, standing and seated near a small table with a white tablecloth on it. All were dressed in their finest, and there was the Chef Cir, the fat politician whose father, it turned out, had been Chief of this very village. In other words we figured that since he had missed the proceedings the day before, having been delayed by affairs of state in Palimé, he had convened everybody to go through the whole thing again under his aegis this time. We explained to him that we had a tight schedule and that we could not possibly stay.

"Oh," said he, "but they want to present you with a lamb."

"All right," we said, "but it will have to be speedy." So there were a few more speeches and I took a picture of the group with my Polaroid camera, which I gave to the Chief, and everyone was happy.

The Chef Cir accompanied us to the frontier of his territory, about two hours' drive away where we were met by the Chef Cir of Akposso who took over from there. In the end, this one turned out to be a very good friend who later came to our house in Lomé twice. He was accompanied by a PCV, Martha Jean Shaver, who was working in public health all by herself in a little hamlet that we visited later on.

The first place they took us was a school at Amlame, a huge agriculture school with 250 pupils built with "self-help" funds. Here we had the most elaborate and carefully prepared reception of the trip, although meticulousness characterized everything that our new host did throughout our stay with him. All the students and many school children were arrayed in front of the building as well as the faculty and at least two hundred parents. The school singing group performed, and there were more speeches. The Ambassador's talk was very well received. We had been seated on the porch of the school until this time where we could see the dignitaries but not the children. Bud asked if we could walk down in front of the school where he could face them and be seen. His speech ended by his saying that if the United States gave money to build schools in Togo and that if he promised to work as hard as he could to get them the money they needed to expand their school, the children must promise him that they would study hard and make the most of what we provided.

There was wild applause from the faculty and families and everyone was wreathed in smiles when we went into the assembly hall for refreshments. We didn't find out until afterwards that the Chef Cir had declared a holiday in the whole region. On the wall of the assembly hall were photographs of Terence Todman, the DCM (Deputy Chief of Mission of our Embassy) on the occasion of the laying of the cornerstone or whatever it can be called when there really isn't any stone. On the blackboard to the left, drawn in colored chalk, was a map of Togo and a map of the United States (both maps, by the way, were the same size) connected by two outstretched hands, one hairy (the white man) and one not (the black man). To the right were the flags of both countries branching out from a common staff. These as well as the maps were drawn with the greatest of care and exactness. The faculty members with whom I sat to have a glass of beer (Johnny Walker Red Label was also offered at every stop we made even at eight o'clock in the morning) said that the students had done it.

On the way to Atakpame (in Ewe k and p are pronounced together, as are g and b, as one sound, one with the throat and one with the lips. This is hard to do; try it!) we stopped at Koutoukba, Martha Jean's village where there were more ceremonies and more drinks. Martha Jean had learned the local dialect, which, even though it is not Ewe, allows the people to understand Ewe. This we found to be true everywhere which was lucky. As Mr. Jondoh spoke good English, excellent French and perfect Ewe but no dialects, he was able to interpret for us whenever necessary. Martha Jean worked almost exclusively with the women giving talks on hygiene and child care. She worked with the midwife and obviously was much beloved and respected in the village.

In Atakpame we went right to the Chef Cir's house for lunch. By that time it was 12:30 and even though the

morning had been punctuated with any number of libations
we were hungry. Running water was also a treat. The
Chef's wife was a very pretty young woman, the mother of
five children, who spoke excellent French and had a fine
sense of humor. She was as relaxed and easygoing as her
husband was high-strung. (He, by the way, was the fourth-
ranked tennis player in Togo.) Their house consisted of one
good-sized central room with bedrooms off it. We sat there
for drinks before lunch and then went out to a porch in the
back where a long table was set for lunch. What we looked
at during lunch couldn't be called a garden or even a yard
because nothing was growing in it. I guess it would have to
be called a barnyard, although most of what that connotes
was not in evidence. It was surrounded by a hedge of
papyrus and contained a fascinating variety of animals that
provided a floor show. The chickens and sheep minded
their business while the monkey and the dog circulated
about making trouble. It was a delightful lunch. Although
I was filled up by the first course, cold vegetable salad and
stuffed eggs, there were at least five more. One was chick-
en with vegetables, and two were meat courses including
goat. As usual I found them quite unchewable, although
not unpalatable, while the Africans guzzled it all down with
no trouble.

In the afternoon, the Chef Cir took us to see four PCV's
in a very poor village called Otadi. Being a clever man, he
had the driver stop on the way at a maternity clinic, which
had been constructed six years ago. Although the building
was fine, it had only a matrone in charge, almost no med-
ications, and not even any beds. We saw one woman whose
baby was expected to be delivered that night lying on the
floor with her other child beside her. They were covered

only by her shawl. We decided Susan's Christmas present that year would be eight beds for that place donated by her father and me. We hoped she wouldn't mind.

In Otadi we came first upon a big, blond he-man PCV building a house with the help of some village friends for himself and his bride, the Peace Corps nurse in the village, whom he was to marry in a few months. He explained that the house would be round with a thatched roof. It would be made of bricks, which were easily produced from a combination of nine parts indigenous laterite soil and one part cement. As a result, he would be using very few bags of cement in the whole house.

We went to the house of the Chief of the village, a gnarled old boy, who had been in office since the "temps des Allemands". While we were talking to him, three Peace Corps girls came in to meet us. Besides the nurse, there were two public health workers who ran a clinic and traveled around the countryside on their motor scooters giving health talks. Afterwards we learned that the Chef de Canton (another administrative rank of the central government appointed in Lomé) had given the girls a goat and a lot of fou-fou, and I don't know what else so that they could entertain us at dinner that night. When the girls discovered that we had no time to stop for dinner, they tried to return these gifts to the chief, but he refused to accept them. We wrote him a letter, which we hoped would relay to him how flattered we were.

By this time it was almost dark and we started down to Atakpame. When we got to the village where the deserted hospital was that I described, we encountered a great delegation in the road. It was the Chief of the village who wished to present us two chickens, a large number of oranges, and some rice. These we accepted graciously; I took a picture with my Polaroid which fortunately has a flash and left it with the Chief, and we were on our way again. All the way back to town oranges rolled around under our feet and the chickens protested their bondage.

We were glad to get back to our rooms in time to have a little drink before dinner. Luckily, the excellent thermos, which Albert had purchased in Washington, still contained some ice. The only bitter note was that all running water in Atakpame was turned off for repairs, so we didn't have the shower we had been looking forward to. We managed to get clean enough in a nice bucket provided by the "management." Our rooms were in an enormous spooky old house, which was used by the Chef Cir to house VIP's. We called it Blair House. Unlike the campement in Palimé, this one hadn't even been cleaned since General Ludendorff's last visit. Unlike Poland, however, it wasn't sordid. Nothing smelled and the dirt was just dust, not filth. The old man who was the caretaker perceived that I liked flowers and each day filled the room with fresh bouquets, which, for me, could always take the sting out of anything.

We dined at the Chef Cir's house, this time alone with his wife and Mr. Jondoh. We stayed much too late, but the conversation about his history (he was a school teacher for ten years before joining the government, and was still only thirty-five), his work, his hopes for the future, political problems in Togo, and a half dozen other subjects was too good to let go.

The next day might be referred to as "The Longest Week." We left Atakpame at 7:30 a.m. in the Chef Cir's Land Rover with our car following along behind. Both cars were *full* of people. In the Land Rover was the Ambassador and Mr. Jondoh – front seat; Martha Jean, the Chef Cir, and I – second seat; a uniformed policeman with a rifle, the Chief of the Press and Information Service of Akposso, and a charming young male English teacher who had studied at the University of San José in California on a grant from the Afro-American Institute – in the "way" back. Soon we were joined by a police escort, two beautiful gentlemen who preceded us in a blue jeep in order to stop cars coming the other way so that we could get through without delay.

The road was narrow and very bumpy and we drove like lightning. The police escort was an asset, except for the laterite dust which was a natural consequence and which turned my hair orange. I don't know what color the inside of my trachea was when it was all over, but I do know that I had a lot of new muscles in my arms from holding on tightly to the bar handle fortunately provided in front of each seat in the Land Rover.

Our first stop was at a self-help dispensary project at Okou. The building was splendid and coming along nicely. The medical staff, the Chef Cir assured us, even existed. We would be invited back for the dedication the next month.

In Kougnobou we stopped for a visit with an American missionary couple, Jim Winters and his wife, who were doing agricultural development not unlike the monks with funds that came from the United Church of Christ. We liked them very much, and besides they gave us a cold drink and let us use the most ingenious latrine in the world, which I would be happy to describe separately to anyone interested.

It was 10:30 by the time we arrived at Badou, where we were met by the Chef de Poste (an administrative job under the Chef Cir) and a large delegation of elders. By this time we were very near the Ghana border so we found many more English speakers. One of these was the Chief of the village who explained to me that had it not been market day that day, all the villagers would have turned out as well. Speeches were exchanged in the "palaver" hut. There we learned that the much beloved Chef de Canton had died a month before and that we would be taken to see his house and the place where he is buried. What happened next was one of the truly unforgettable dramas of the trip. We piled back into our cars again, but this time much more crowded because a number of dignitaries wished to accompany us. An additional group went by foot and met us at the impressive dwelling of the deceased Chef.

We were ushered into a hallway and through that into a courtyard, three sides of which were formed by the house, the fourth being a series of little rooms (kind of like a motel) one story high. Out of each one of these rooms emerged a wife, or rather a widow, some with little children in their arms or tugging at their skirts. They were all dressed in the same fabric, a bright red print, which I assumed had no particular significance or connection with the death of their late husband. They were said to be five in number, but it seemed to me that there were more than that. In any case, they were of assorted ages and even though the Chef was only fifty-seven, one of them looked about a hundred and twenty. We shook hands with each of them. They were obviously very sad, and from looking at the photograph of the event, so were we. We proceeded to the grave, which, of all things, was inside the house. A hole had been dug in the cement floor of one of the rooms, the Chef buried in it, and the top cemented over again. There was a picture of the Chef hanging on the wall and a candle burning at each corner of the grave. It was as grim as grim can be, and we had not been prepared for it.

To get out of the house to where our cars were, we had to pass through the courtyard again. By this time the wives and their retinues had set up such a wailing that we were shaken.

Lunch, at the residence of the Chef de Poste in Badou, preceded a visit to the frontier station between Togo and Ghana. The Chef Cir was determined to show us every inch of his territory, and he did. The interesting part of the tour of the customs and other facets of the border station was the behavior of the officials. Suddenly we came upon people who were trying to emulate Englishmen instead of Frenchmen. The sergeant major that showed us around carried a swagger stick which he used to open doors, point to his police dogs, move a stone out of the path, scratch his leg, and anything else he could think of to ease his nervousness. His uniform, his bearing, his moustache were as nearly English as he could make them and he took himself very seriously.

In Tomegbe, our next stop, we visited some French nursing sisters who had established a crude but very useful maternity clinic and hospital. We visited the rooms and saw some of the babies who were very clean and peaceful lying by their mothers in little handmade cots. They had trained some African assistants without whom they say they could not manage. We were there on a clinic day, and the place was jammed. We visited the mission high school, run by French priests where a charming Peace Corps girl was teaching English.

Tomegbe is the cocoa capital of the region. When we went to the "palaver" hut for speeches we were presented with five huge fruits of the cocoa tree, some yellow and some green, which represented two kinds of cocoa, one that had been imported from Brazil and one from Ghana. We cut one open and sucked on the beans inside which had a white sweet coat on them, were moist and tasted only faintly of chocolate. The beans were left in the sunshine in a closed container to ferment for three days and then were spread on a large tarpaulin to dry. I never found out what happened to them after that, but I imagined that they were bagged in sacks that people could carry on their backs to a central location where they were prepared for further refining in Ghana.

At three o'clock we left Badou for Atakpame taking a different road. The Chef Cir particularly wanted us to see this road because it was maintained by the people of the region at his urging without any outside help. It might not sound like an extraordinary thing to do, but we saw precious few examples of that kind of initiative. Obviously, it could be done. There were just very few leaders like our friend. The second reason for taking that particular road was that it went through the hometown of the Chef Cir, and he wanted us to meet his parents. We were thankful afterwards that he did that because it gave us a small idea of how at least one African family has progressed in the last generation. His mother and father live in an adobe and grass hut, one room with a dirt floor. They cooked with charcoal on a stove made of rocks. If I thought the wife of the deceased Chef was over a hundred, then this lady had to be in her second century. Obviously our friend, the Chef Cir, was a Benjamin (born late). I took a family picture with my Polaroid, which I presented to the mother; the Chief of the village presented us with a lamb, and we piled back into our vehicles with our entourage including the ever-vigilant police escort. Not once in Togo did we feel threatened. The escort was a gesture of courtesy, nothing more.

At six-thirty we were back at Blair House where we took Martha Jean Shaver for a glass of hot sherry which by that time was all we had left in the way of liquid refreshment; well, not counting our case of bottled water which held out nicely until we got home. The bath water was turned on at Blair House that evening so we each in turn reveled in the luxury of a shower. This was preparation for a dinner hosted by us at the hotel in Atakpame in honor of the Chef Cir, his wife, and a committee of three gentlemen known as the Special Delegation who advised him on how to run the Circonscription. In addition at the table there was the local Information man who accompanied us on all our travels in Akposso, and Martha Jean. It was a long table and there were some good toasts to our health and safety, and lots of French wine. We even danced after dinner on the terrace of the hotel to recorded music - European - creating an exquisite surreal atmosphere.

The next day was devoted to seeing the sights of the Circonscription of Atakpame. As the Chef Cir himself had been ill, we were accompanied by his secretary, who turned out to be a cousin of Mr. Jondoh. That, however, didn't loosen his tongue at all and his shyness persisted. We had the company of the press man again who was a nice fellow. By then we had become quite attached to him.

We toured the city of Atakpame, visiting yet another convent mission school where there were two Peace Corps people teaching. What I found most interesting was the chapel, which was made entirely of materials found in the region and decorated by artists of the region. There was a touching primitive Madonna and child made, I gathered, by the local mason in his spare time. The insides of the louvers in the plaster walls were painted pastel colors so that all around the top of the church where the louvers were letting in air, the light was slightly colored almost as though it were coming in through stained glass.

The national normal school was in Atakpame. Students from all over Togo who wanted to train to be teachers got their higher education there. I saw the young women's boarding department, which was spic and span to the last detail. The director of the school happened to mention that he had written to the Embassy to see whether we could provide reading material on the United States. As we had the back of our truck well stocked, the Ambassador was able to make his presentation on the spot.

At 10:30 we started for Kolokpoe where the French had an experimental cotton farm. This turned out to be not only instructive but also very pleasant as the director of the farm gave us a very good French lunch at his house. Before the luncheon, we toured the establishment, trying to ask intelligent questions. What we knew about different strains of cotton was limited, but we didn't know until then how limited. They had bought a small herd of cows a few years earlier in order to have a fertilizer supply. These cows, feeding on the legumes that were planted in the resting fields, had multiplied so that the herd numbered 350 beasts. The herders were instructed to drive the cows out of the tall bean plants so we could see them. They finally did so with some degree of difficulty, creating a very un-African scene. It looked more like Texas: a huge herd with a background of good healthy cotton. The only criticism of the operation there was that it had taken so long. The French had been working for twenty years in that place, and they were only then coming up with a superior type of cotton adapted to the region and the methods of farming employed by the Africans.

In the afternoon we visited a textile mill, a private corporation under German management, which was producing stunning cottons for local consumption and for export. I was delighted to have the opportunity to make personal contact with the manager, as I was counting on them to provide some suitable fabrics for our use in an imaginary enterprise, a wild conception that had been growing in my head throughout the trip. He said they would make special dye lots for us, and I assumed he would sell to us at wholesale prices. I planned to go back when we had found a definite location for a shop.

We returned to Blair House just in time to freshen up for a dinner we gave at the hotel for the Peace Corps people we had met in the area. The Chef Cir and his wife came too. We were fifteen at the table and it was jolly. The table looked pretty, decorated with three enormous bouquets we found in our room when we returned from our day in the country. We had stopped at the hotel before starting our rounds to order a special menu. It turned out to be more or less what we had in mind, but I was not surprised that they were psychologically incapable of serving the salad and the meat course at the same time, which of course, would also cause a problem for a Frenchman.

En route home the next day we stopped at Nuatja where we met another Chef Cir; the elders gathered for speeches. We heard a lot about the "ver de Guinée" and a heartrending tale about the well they had just dug and the pump which was not strong enough to pump the water up. They had just discovered this the day before we arrived and the Chef Cir confided that he did not know how to tell the people that their back-breaking labor had been in vain. The Ambassador promised to try to help them, but that, of course, it all depended on how the Congress finally treated the AID appropriations still pending. It was like a broken record.

When we retired to the residence of the Chef Cir with some of the big shots, I sat next to the biggest of them all whose outfit should be described for history. His leather sandals were exceedingly handsome, each decorated with a beast that looked like a dinosaur carved out of ebony. The thing about the dinosaur was that he was sewn onto the sandals standing up and facing away from the wearer. Doubtless they would be protection against almost anything. His robes were made of especially elegant material. His fingers were laden with gold rings. There was a long heavy gold chain around his neck, which had hanging from it miniature garden tools made of silver. On the top of his head, brand clean and neatly folded into a ten-inch square, was a thick black towel which, I was told, kept his ideas from escaping.

It was after a couple of similar but less ambitious trips that I cranked up the nerve to go to the Minister of Commerce for permission to try my hand at doing something viable with the work I had seen. I told him I would like to open a shop, that the original investment would come from private sources (me and whomever I could convince to take a chance just for fun), I would never take any profit myself and should my idea develop satisfactorily, I would gift the result to the Togolese government to run as a national enterprise.

The Minister looked stunned. After absorbing the fact that there would be no expense or responsibility accruing to his department or to him personally, he gave his consent without hesitation, but I didn't think for a minute that he expected ever to hear of it again. I was quite stunned myself as I drove away realizing finally what an agenda I had set for myself.

Fairly quickly, however, the basic pieces did fall into place. It went like this: the Embassy had a building which housed the little international school upstairs over what was called the "transient apartment" where no one had ever wanted to stay because it was so close (just a few meters) from the main road connecting Accra, the capital of Ghana, and Lagos, capital of Nigeria. The beach, also a thorough-fare, was just across the road and there was a certain amount of foot traffic and a lot of night life. When I asked the ambassador's permission to put this space to use, he agreed, and luckily there were State Department inspectors in town who blessed the project and the use of the property.

We started designing clothes right away made from the beautiful fabrics we found in the central market. We hired a seamstress to start with a borrowed sewing machine making long flowing dresses and pants suits, which were stylish at the time. With the help of the Peace Corps and my own collecting we acquired enough stock to open the doors. In the meantime I had had an enormous sign constructed and mounted outside right next to the road alerting passers by to the existence of "Boutique Togo à Gogo" executed in the colors of the Togolese flag.

It worked. People driving along that road stopped and bought things. The only trouble was that in about a week's time we were completely sold out and had to close the doors for major restocking and redecorating. My colleagues among the embassy ladies who had worked hard were delighted with this result and were full of creative ideas, which we tried to realize as we went about the next step. We decorated the interior with a motif reminiscent of village architecture with small pointed palm frond roofs covering the racks of clothing. We used branches to make an interesting display for jewelry. We hired several seamstresses and borrowed as many sewing machines as we could, replacing them later with new ones as we began to have profits. The seamstresses all sat together in one large room, which had been a bedroom in the apartment. A smaller one was divided in two to make fitting rooms. And the old sofa and matching chairs we found in the place were reupholstered with fabric from the local textile mill.

Everything looked fresh and, we thought, spectacular. We advertised in *Togo Presse*, the local newspaper, for young fashion models and held our breath. The girls who turned up were more or less qualified, maybe not Suzy Parker, but we explained what we wanted them to do and had a rehearsal. We had to rely on embassy staff to rig up electricity and a public address system in the shop's small garden where a runway was constructed.

We managed the publicity by ourselves in a clumsy fashion, but on opening night an overflow crowd attended our outdoor fashion show. The girls performed like champs and I had a chance to explain to the public what our aims were. The French population thought the idea was amusing but absolutely impractical because the local people were bound to make it fail somehow. We couldn't believe them. After we had been in business for a couple of months, we had a surprise boost from the *New York Times*. A correspondent named Gloria Emerson was roaming around West Africa looking for a story to write. One of my friends in the embassy in Dakar, Senegal, told her about Togo à GoGo and suggested it could be the subject of an interesting article. So Gloria, whom I finally met fifty years later when we were both old ladies, wrote the story, which gave us the connection we most needed.

One morning I came down to breakfast and found a pile of letters eight inches high each containing a check for fifteen dollars and an order for "one of your lovely caftans". I didn't know then what a caftan was, but from the description in the dictionary I designed something I thought might satisfy, as long as we loaded it with enough machine embroidery typical of our area to be impressive. Gloria had even set the price for us, which we were able to stick to and still make a small profit. One woman told me she had a purple sofa to take into account and another informed me of the coloring of her dog. So we were suddenly hurled into the mail order business. We decided as much as possible to use only materials made in Togo. We could find everything we needed right there except paper, zippers, and most important, labels to sew inside the garments. I went to Ghana to buy paper bags for shipping the orders and for zippers, but labels came from Cincinnati.

There was a screened porch attached to our building which we had not utilized until business became so active that we needed something for our clients to do while waiting their turn for a fitting or other service. So we made a tearoom there and hired a man to handle that side of the business. Meanwhile, we put our two garages to use, one for carpenters making small pieces of furniture from African teak, like the spoon chairs I had seen in Palimé, and interesting little tables with animal motifs for pedestals. Teak in Africa is a smaller tree than it is in Asia where the enormous salad bowls we see everywhere come from. There was, therefore, a limit to the types of things our men could make but soon we had salad utensils and other items appropriate for "gifts from Africa".

The other garage housed the embroiderers, all men who came to us bringing their own machines. Once a year we were invited to put on a fashion show for the directors of the phosphate mining company. These gentlemen and their wives were mostly French, being entertained by the company at dinner at the Israeli-built hotel. We looked forward to these events avidly because they generated what seemed to us like an enormous volume of sales and the lavish compliments were good for our morale and our reputation. We tried to use every opportunity to increase sales. For example, when there was a courtesy visit by an American battleship, the U.S.S. *Dahlgren*, one of the Embassy wives took a huge box of embroidered African shirts we had prepared in advance to the dock where she sold every one in an hour.

I regretted that we were not yet making neckties from African fabrics. I dissected one of my husband's ties to make a pattern which I distributed to women who came in looking for work, along with an adequate amount of material which they could take home and bring back finished. They all succeeded on the first try, but after that the ties became gradually more "original" so we couldn't use them. It was understandable, since they had no idea what a necktie was. That was my fault, not theirs, and when it was corrected, the neckties were popular though absurdly wild. A buyer from Denmark came by about every three months to pick up his order. What did they look like walking down the streets of Copenhagen?

Our sales staff consisted of embassy wives, the wife of the head of Oxfam, and a beautiful Togolese woman who was the chief cutter in the sewing room and a good model, being tall and thin which was not the typical shape of the Ewe women who were predominant along the coast where we were. It was a blessing to have Susan, my daughter, and a friend arrive for the summer. I pressed them into service as they both spoke passable French and were quick learners. All along I kept my eyes and ears open for more Togolese possibilities for sales, finally finding one person, a well-educated young woman to whom I fancied I could turn over the responsibility of the showroom when I had to leave.

I made several trips to Washington to convince the Peace Corps to send someone to supervise, which I finally succeeded in doing. Their hesitance was based on the fact that we sold very little to Africans. The mayor of Lomé at the time was a woman who became a friend for whom we made a couple of splendid outfits and when the President of Congo, the dreaded Mobuto Sese Seko, came for an official visit, his wife made an order, but she never paid. She owes me thirty-eight dollars, which I resent to this day. Both she and her husband were serious believers in what I call "snoblesse oblige", a reflection of the old tribal village organization which has generally been the undoing of all the newly independent countries of West Africa.

In Washington for a short consultation about a year later we were honored to have the Togolese ambassador give a party to which we were invited which was reported in the *Washington Star* as an outstanding social event where the main topic of conversation was Boutique Togo à Gogo. The article caught the attention of Clark Mollenhof, a journalist, who had been appointed to the White House staff by President Nixon to ferret out wrongdoing in the Executive Branch, which seems more misdirected now even than it did at the time in view of what came later at that White House. Copies of Mr. Mollenhof's letter to the State Department, and the return reply are included in the following pages. This little fracas caused the Bureau of African Affairs (AF) a lot of trouble. As Mr. Pederson (a political appointee, serving as Counselor to the State Department, who had perhaps imagined when he accepted the post that he would be engaged in high-level wrangling between governments) explained in an exasperated tone when we finally met at a luncheon in Kinshasa during a meeting of U.S. ambassadors to West African nations, "I have spent my entire time in Washington defending you."

THE EVENING STAR
Washington, D.C.
Tuesday, September 27, 1969

'Togo-a-Gogo'
Shop a Big Topic

The success of "Togo-A-Gogo," a swinging boutique opened last year in Togo by the wife of the U.S. Ambassador there, was a big topic of conversation last night at the Togo Embassy.

The U.S. career diplomat, Albert W. Sherer, now back in this country to work on the State Department selections board, attended the party with his wife, who talked enthusiastically about her boutique. Mrs. Alexandre Ohin, wife of the Togo ambassador, showed several hostess dresses from the shop.

Last night's party was in honor of Togo Minister of Foreign Affairs Joachim Hunlede, who has been in this country attending the U.N. General Assembly.

DEPARTMENT OF STATE

Washington, D.C. 20520

LIMITED OFFICIAL USE   October 21, 1969

MEMORANDUM

TO   : C - Mr. Pedersen

THROUGH: S/S

FROM   : AF - David D. Newsom

SUBJECT: Letter from Mr. Clark R. Mollenhoff, Deputy Counsel to the
          President - ACTION MEMORANDUM

     An article in the <u>Evening Star</u> of September 30, 1969, concerning
a community project originated by Mrs. Albert Sherer, wife of our
Ambassador to Togo, brought an inquiry from Mr. Clark R. Mollenhoff,
Deputy Counsel to the President. The article may have implied that
Mrs. Sherer was in business for herself. In fact, she and other Embassy
wives have worked tirelessly to create a marketing mechanism for the
benefit of the local community, an activity clearly in the best interests
of the United States. The history and goals of the business in question
have all been explained in the attached letter to Mr. Mollenhoff, which
is submitted to you for your signature.

Recommendation

     That you sign the attached letter to Mr. Mollenhoff (Tab A).

Attachments:

    Tab A - Letter to Mr. Mollenhoff

    Tab B - Letter from Mr. Mollenhoff of October 3, 1969

AF/W-WSC:jwt 10/21/69   Cleared: AF/W - Mr. Melbourne
    Ext. 23066   DG/PER - Mr. Sohm
                                                       (Acting)

                LIMITED OFFICIAL USE

DEPARTMENT OF STATE
THE LEGAL ADVISER

MEMORANDUM   November 4, 1969

To: C - Mr. Richard F. Pedersen

From: L - John R. Stevenson

Subject: Letter from Mr. Clark R. Mollenhoff concerning
         Mrs. Sherer's Participation in a Venture in Togo

I concur in the attached letter to Clark Mollenhoff and
have added my clearance on Assistant Secretary Newsom's
transmittal memorandum to you.

Mr. Lyerly of this office has worked closely with AF
on this matter and assisted in drafting the final letter
attached.

While the facts indicate that the ladies in Togo became
"interested" in a business in their country of assignment without the express approval as required by the
Department's regulations, it is quite clear that the
Ambassador and the Assistant Secretary for AF endorsed
the project.

Attachment

S/S - 16244

Copies To:
U
J
C
S/FC
AF
AF/W
L
L/O
L/A F
DG/PER
S/S-S:CMS

NOV 5 1969

DEPARTMENT OF STATE
WASHINGTON

November 5, 1969

Dear Mr. Mollenhoff:

I was pleased to receive your letter of October 3, because of the opportunity it provided to correct any misconceptions that might have arisen from the Evening Star article of September 30, concerning the Boutique Togo-A-Gogo. The Evening Star article did not make clear that the participation of Mrs. Sherer, wife of our Ambassador to Togo, in the shop is a strictly voluntary activity in which neither she nor any other American makes a profit. Although our investigation has established that Mrs. Sherer's participation in the project may appear to be in technical conflict with certain State Department regulations, it is clear that her interest is totally without any prospect of gainful return, and in our belief, it has furthered U.S. national interests in Togo.

The short history of the Boutique is a tribute to the resourcefulness and sense of responsibility of our American diplomatic representation in Togo. Shortly after the arrival of Ambassador and Mrs. Sherer in Togo, while on a short orientation tour in northern Togo, the Sherers noted examples of fine African handicraft and needlework for sale in the village marketplaces, where the demand for such manufactures is limited by the low economic levels prevalent in the rural environment. It appeared that one of the prime problems for the peasant handicrafter was a lack of adequate marketing channels.

In response to this need, Mrs. Sherer and four other Embassy wives formed the American Society for the Development of Togolese Arts and Crafts, which included in its charter the intention to open a small shop in Lome to serve as a marketing center for Togolese arts and crafts. An initial contribution of $2,000 was made by the Sherers and other Embassy personnel in the early part of 1968 (the boutique opened on June 12, 1968). At such time that adequate cash surplus is available, this money will be returned to the contributors. A Board of Directors was established which included one French woman (wife of the general manager of the phosphate mine), one Swiss, seven Togolese and two Americans. The Togolese included Mrs. Sivomey, the lady mayor of

Mr. Clark R. Mollenhoff,
    Deputy Counsel to the President,
        The White House.

continued on next page

-2-

Lome, Mr. Ayivor (Togolese Director of Tourism), Mrs. Jondoh (a prominent wholesaler of fabrics), Mr. Hadzi (representing the Chamber of Commerce), Mr. Kponton (head of the National Museum), and Mrs. Trenou, Administrative Secretary General of the Chamber of Commerce.

The legal status of the nonprofit society is unclear. It appears that it operates at the present time with the tacit consent of the Togolese Government. As you have previously noted, the Board of Directors includes members representing the most important government ministries and the private sector. I have been informed that the wives of the Foreign Minister and the French Ambassador also take a strong interest.

During the course of the development of the enterprise, the Ambassador kept the Department fully informed of the Society's plans. Clearance for the project has been indicated in several letters to the Ambassador from Joseph Palmer, then Assistant Secretary of State for African Affairs.

As a result of the energies and acumen of the various Embassy wives and their foreign and Togolese collaborators, the shop has made a good beginning. It provides full-time employment for 15 seamstresses and provides a ready marketplace for several dozen other local artisans who might not otherwise benefit from the steady income which the shop provides. Most of the shop's income, to the present time, has been expended on salaries and in improving the productive capacity of the enterprise. Hard currency sales, for example, have allowed the organization to purchase sewing machinery from the United States. No U.S. Government funds have ever been allocated to the Society. At such time that the boutique's income exceeds the cost of operation the proceeds will be put into Togolese welfare activities.

Visitors to the boutique report that it is situated in a small and neat bungalow on the main ocean front highway in Lome. The articles are displayed with taste and imagination. The building is rented from a Togolese citizen.

The Embassy women now serve primarily as supervisors to the seamstresses and as advisors to the other artisans in order to provide expertise on styling and quality control. Mrs. Sherer and the other Embassy wives have unselfishly contributed an average of five hours a day to the success of the boutique without any other remuneration other than the satisfaction that comes from helping people to help themselves. Because of the growing size of the operation, the Embassy wives are planning gradually to phase out their time-consuming participation in the project, with the hope that the Peace Corps might be able to provide interim management assistance. The ultimate goal of the founders is to turn the entire operation over to the Togolese, when adequate personnel are trained.

-3-

Our investigation has revealed an unclear aspect of the Embassy wive involvement in the organization related to the possible issue of diplomat immunity should this arise. Accordingly, we plan to request that no official American or dependent be represented on the Board of Directors. We believe that the ladies will agree with this action as a desire on the part of the Department to avoid any possible conflict that could arise out of the unincorporated nature of the shop. We are going to advise the Embassy to use its influence with the Board to clarify the organization's status under Togolese law, since in the event of a lawsuit against the shop, it appears that all of the current principals might be personally liable.

I have spoken about your letter to Ambassador Sherer, who is in Washington, D. C., serving on the Selection Boards of the Foreign Service. He has stated his willingness to discuss this matter with you if you have any additional questions.

Sincerely yours,

Richard F. Pedersen

Richard F. Pedersen
Counselor

AF/W-WCCrorke:lsr/jwt 10/16/69 - 10/24/69
Clearances: AF/W - Amb. Sherer
             AF - Mr. Newsom
             L/O - Mr. Lyerly
             L/AF - Mr. Runyon
             S/S -

As time went on and the Boutique continued to have orders from abroad, I became curious enough to pack a small suitcase full of samples to take to the U.S. to see if I could do any direct selling to department stores. I had never done anything in my life like that, which was probably an asset because if I had, it would have meant correspondence and more time than we had. I simply walked in to the department where I thought our dresses would sell best and asked to see the buyer. Several orders were generated in this way, but few reorders. The buyers complained because our goods were not plastic-wrapped and we had no way of attaching price tags in advance.

We were making modest profit all the time, which I deposited in one of our two bank accounts, one in African francs in the French bank in Lomé and one in American dollars in the Chicago bank I had used all my life. When we were transferred away, I left these two accounts - which by then came to several thousand dollars each - in the care of a young man, an employee of the Bureau de Tourism, who in the long run turned out to have no business sense at all, even though the Peace Corps had by that time sent two volunteers, one a designer and one a business school graduate.

I am still in touch with the beautiful woman who was the chief cutter in the atelier who tells me that for starters the shop was moved after I left to a new location on the second floor of a dingy interior street. And I never asked, but surely no one from the boutique went at least once a week to renew the contents of the showcase in the important hotel, the only place for traveling businessmen, a token from the Israelis who wooed small African countries as did the Taiwanese in hopes of getting their vote at the U.N.

Throughout all this, our residence hummed along

smoothly with only a couple of minor episodes, which straightened themselves out promptly. One was over a blouse of mine that had gone missing, I thought. I asked Bernadette to find it for me since she was the laundress and our chambermaid, an extremely meticulous person. She was also beautiful, the only female domestic servant I ever knew in West Africa. I trusted her completely, but I trusted them all: three housemen, four gardeners, and the chef whose French name was Apollinaire (which I liked). Certainly all those people changed back to their African names as soon as they perceived that their employment depended only on the quality of their work. Bernadette looked everywhere but couldn't find the blouse. Soon, because of the blouse and who might know about it, the air in the house became too stiff and tense to be tolerated. My sweet household was out of order. So I called Ambrose, the Togolese member of the embassy staff responsible for hiring and firing and generally dealing with problems concerning local employees. I told him about the problem and asked him to come out to a meeting of everyone on the place, which he did the next day.

We all stood around in a group on the porch while he explained that I had decided to give them three days to find the blouse. If the blouse was not found in that length of time, everyone would be fired. He added that they all knew how old I was because they had seen my children. I guess that provided testimony to the fact that I knew what I was doing.

At this moment Robert stepped forward and asked if he might make a suggestion. Of course I welcomed that. His suggestion was that if at the end of three days, the blouse had not turned up they be permitted to call a "fetisheur" (a magic man). All heads nodded. There was no doubt that the fetisheur would tell us where to look for the blouse. I agreed to that suggestion immediately and for two days I entertained the fond hope that a magic man would be necessary. I thought he would set up a holy site composed of his particular selection of power items like small bird bones, a rag or two, an enchanted stick (I had seen these and much more for sale in markets all over the country) and over his construction he would pour a certain amount of gin while chanting magic words. At the conclusion of his ceremony we would know where to find the blouse and how it got there. I was very eager to have all this happen on our place. I wondered if I would be permitted to attend.

However, to my disappointment, the next afternoon when I went to the garage to go to work at the shop, there was the blouse on the roof of my car. I quietly handed the blouse to Bernadette who made no comment, and no word, that I heard anyway, was ever spoken about the episode again. Everyone went back to work as though nothing had happened. One is never far away from magic in Africa.

There is an explanation for everything that happens. For example, the morning after Apollo 11, the first moon flight when Neil Armstrong walked around up there, there was a plague of conjunctivitis in Lomé, which only seemed to affect the local population. It quickly assumed the name "Apollo Onze" because everyone knows that humans are not allowed on the moon. This must be somewhere in the Koran. But the whole town believed it, and believed it whether they were Muslim or not.

About a year after arriving in Togo, we had a surprise. At the end of October 1968, President Johnson assigned to

Albert a second simultaneous ambassadorship, Equatorial Guinea, a newly independent ex-Spanish colony. It is divided into two distinct parts, one an island off the coast of Nigeria called Fernando Po, inhabited by a tribe called the Fangs, and the other just opposite it on the mainland called Rio Muni, inhabited by the Bubis. These nubbins of African real estate, inhabited by two different tribes speaking different languages, were said to have no love for each other. I was looking forward to seeing more of this strange continent full of surprises when Albert presented his credentials to the new government, but to my regret I was unable to accompany him because of big doings at the shop, a fashion show for the key personnel of the mining company.

Afterwards he recounted the incredible event of his swearing-in like this: A plane had been chartered in Douala, (a city in neighboring Cameroon we always had to go through to get to Equatorial Guinea) to take him across the small expanse of water between there and the island capitol, Fernando Po. The weather was not favorable, but since he knew that a ceremony was being arranged on the other end, he went ahead. This was the only time I remember that his knowing how to fly a plane was a genuine mercy. The storm was so violent after they got up there in the clouds that Albert had to take the co-pilot's seat and help with brute force to keep the plane from going into a spin. He perspired so profusely that, by his own description, he was soaked through by the time he arrived on the ground in Fernando Po.

The State Department had told him that regular business attire was all that was required, so he had to apologize several times to the Chief of Protocol who was exasperated anyway because the plane arrived so late and on top of that kept asking, "Donde esta su gala?" (Where is your mourning coat?). True, that is the uniform usually prescribed for presentation of credentials ceremonies, at least in Europe, and since Albert was the first ambassador to be invited to present, formal Spanish protocol was prescribed. Too bad! Finally Spanish champagne was served, which caused everyone to perspire more. But diplomats follow certain traditions, which in many cases serve to break the ice or fire between people who have not met and whose own customs are miles apart. In this case, the pageant sounded like a flop, but in retrospect I see that it was the opposite.

Three months later we went there together to host a reception with orchestra and dancing at the Paradise Pavilion (a perfect venue for Ginger Rogers and Fred Astaire), and for the list of guests deemed "important" by the Foreign Ministry and personnel of the Mobil offshore rig who entertained us on board, an unforgettable experience. It was seventy-five miles out, off the shore of Port Harcourt, Nigeria, where we were met by helicopter. It was a floating man-made island where seventy-five men lived and worked twelve-hour shifts for stretches of twenty-eight days. At the end of that time they were flown to London or Las Palmas, the destination of their choice, for twelve days of freedom. On the rig no liquor was allowed and everyone was so exhausted from heavy labor that I gather the only other occupation was sleeping or going to whatever movie was being shown in the theater on board.

The rig was its own world. Arrangements for social and other events were made in advance by Al Williams, a Class 3 Foreign Service Officer who had been assigned as Chargé d'Affaires to this brand new country. He was very intelligent and enthusiastic about his post, which added to our curiosity and enjoyment as we went about learning the ropes. The flavor of the place was a contrast to Lomé. The air was silken and sweet as opposed to the loud ocean waves and high winds I had become accustomed to. It felt sparsely populated, probably since the Spaniards had mostly left. The sand on the beach that circled Fernando Po was black because the city was built on volcanic rock. I caught several black sand crabs and put them in a matchbox expecting to create a historic race war back in Lomé, but to my disappointment my challengers all escaped and disappeared in my suitcase.

Al Williams informed me that the wives of the cabinet ministers would like to have a meeting with me. I invited them to come to our hotel room the next day. It turned out that they knew what I was doing in Togo and perhaps were inspired by that to make an unscheduled request. One of them, probably the wife of the Foreign Minister, said they wanted to learn how to set the table properly and how to serve a meal and instruct their servants. I was surprised and flattered, but then even more so when one of them spoke up and said, "We would also like to learn about colors and what to wear." Then another one startled me by adding, "What you don't know is that our grandmothers were wearing skins."

I still am not sure whether that is true or what my face looked like when I received this information. It took me by surprise and I don't remember whether my reply was delayed, but I suppose it was. Finally, I thanked them for their confidence and promised that the next time I came for a visit we would start something. This idea soon disappeared into the miasma of tragic African politics. By the time we returned to Fernando Po (later renamed Bioko) for the celebration of the first year of independence of Equatorial Guinea, all the original government leaders were dead or living in exile. Every six feet along the walls of the cathedral stood a soldier in uniform sporting a Kalashnikov at the ready.

The anniversary weekend was too strange to be believed, but we attended every event - including a bullfight at 3 a.m. - and learned that the new crowd was even more pretentious and unrealistic than many of the African leaders we already knew. At the official celebratory meal, a buffet in what had formerly been the Spanish governor's palace, guests were discarding their chicken bones and other refuse on the oriental carpets and using the upholstery on the furniture as napkins. Perhaps it was their way of showing contempt for the colonizers. I got into an unwelcome discussion with Diallo Telli, later head of the OAU (Organization of African Unity), who approached me determined to argue about how amazed I would be when Africa turned out to be able to develop itself to new heights of civilization and power that he knew I could not imagine. And it would happen as a result of African genius and energy alone. I guess he knew what I was trying to do in Lomé and wanted to assure me, in case there was any doubt, that now that they were liberated, Equatorial Guineans would do things their own way.

Diallo Telli was right. The African way was going to be different. Now (2005) that it has been discovered and announced that Equatorial Guinea is floating in oil, we will perhaps see what the difference is. My mind is open. It is still possible.

CHAPTER TWELVE

Heads Down and Chins Up

A FEW MONTHS LATER (1969) Albert was named Ambassador to the Republic of Guinea, a coastal country seven degrees above the equator which means that the climate is less rigorous than in Togo. It was there that the United States, China, and the Soviet Union were playing the most vigorous games to win the allegiance of the host country. I can't say that the name Sékou Touré, "President for Life", meant much to me at the time, but I soon found out that he was a major West African hero figure because he had stood up to De Gaulle in such a vigorous fashion that the frustrated French colonials had disabled all the electrical lines and dumped all the state records into the sea, leaving no guidelines as to how the country worked. Knowing this of course engendered a special sympathy in both of us for the country and its leaders.

It started out so well. Bangoura Karim, Minister of Commerce, along with members of our embassy, came to the airport to meet us. On the way into the city in the car, he said to me, "We hope you will help us make a shop at the airport." I was of course very flattered and pleased and I told him so. Nothing ever came of it. Our house was lovely and the garden a real tropical dream. There were palm trees, mangoes, papaya, and numerous thriving "flame trees", a kind of locust tree. Bougainvillea was everywhere as were poinsettias which bloomed all year round. The view from a generous porch, which extended beyond the living room, reached to the swimming pool, where soon we instituted Sunday open house for the whole staff of the embassy and their children.

It can fairly be said that pool was the saving of us all, as events unfolded. Before the trouble started, we sat beside the pool every evening having drinks like Somerset Maugham characters, and watching the hundreds of fruit bats with their two-foot wingspread fly to the mango groves further up the shore. They came by at 7:30 p.m. as though they had bat watches, always preceded by a single scout. Inside the house there was no need for screens because insects were consumed by the bats, and those that did come in after dark were gobbled up immediately by the little geckos that suddenly made their appearance on the walls above the lamps when the electric lights were turned on in the evening. Because we were so near the equator the daily light quotient was approximately the same all year round. Seasonal differences depended mostly on the amount and duration of the rains which, as in Togo, came in summer when the weather was considered cold by the Guineans and indeed it felt that way because the dampness penetrated everything and everybody.

Aside from the bats and the geckos, the wildlife was familiar to me, everything but the green mamba that was spotted in one of the palm trees curled up in a graceful spiral. The servants were so frightened that they insisted on closing up the house. I knew it must be something fierce.

But I didn't know then that it is indeed one of the most dangerous snakes in the world, with a habitat limited to West Africa. There was a gardener who was terrified. "He has his eye on me," he said, and left for home before the snake could get down from the tree and kill him, which was sure to happen. He could feel it.

Our official and social duties centered largely around the business of the bauxite mines at Boke and Kimbo, 51% of which was owned by The Bauxite Mining Co. of Guinea and operated in partnership by a French company and the Reynolds Aluminum Co. The workers, as far as I knew, were mostly Americans living in a trailer camp on the island of Tamara. Their life was not easy or luxurious, but they were glad to be there because they could save a lot of their income; that is until what ever after was referred to as the "invasion" robbed them of whatever peace of mind they had had. I have copied below the notes I wrote as soon as I could sit at my desk that day or the next.

Sunday, November 22, 1970
This day started very early, three in the morning, but very low-key for me because I had taken a sleeping pill before I went to bed in order to be sure of sleeping soundly the night before the motor trip we were planning the next day with Chris (the Ambassador's aide) to Mamou, Labe, Dalaba, and then coming home again Wednesday night in time to be here for Thanksgiving the next day.

So when Albert woke me to say there was gunfire outside, I responded weakly. It sounded like thunder to me. A couple of small planes flew close to the house. But since the electricity had gone out and we had to have the window open, I did not go back to sleep again and remained conscious of the noise which did not let up at all. At six-thirty Dr. Jassie, the Peace Corps physician, telephoned to say that just as he was leaving his house to attend some German technicians at the request of the German Ambassador, Scott Geary, a Peace Corps volunteer, had come in the door with a couple of what appeared to be minor bullet wounds. Jassie called to ask if he could take Scott to his clinic. Albert said no because it was by then obvious that being out in the street was the most dangerous place to be. Then he called the DCM (Don Norland) who suggested they telephone the staff to make sure that people got the order as quickly as possible to stay home.

We dressed and were in radio communication very quickly. Naturally, we all expected the telephone to go out any minute. By this time it was daylight and the firing which had been coming heavily from both sides of us quieted down to only an occasional rifle shot in the distance. The VOR (local radio station, the Voice of the Revolution) started broadcasting about eight o'clock, informing us that there had been an invasion by Portugese mercenaries, European and African. All comrades were exhorted to take up the arms that had been distributed to them by the Party and fight to defend their country. At no time were there any instructions given, however, as to where to go or what to shoot at.

Albert went to the shore with binoculars, and there were boats in the water just opposite the Camayenne Hotel. He identified one big one as an LST (an old troop landing vessel left over from World War II), working in concert with a couple of smaller boats, some sort of launches with pointed prow and flat stern, not exactly war vessels. They were ferrying people, as were a number of even smaller boats from shore. By this time the deck of the LST was full of

Albert presenting his credentials to Togo President Etienne Eyadema,
October 1967

The ambassador's residence in Lomé, Togo 1968

On the road in Togo with our trusty VW camper, 1968

Albert joins a "handkerchief dance" in the village of
Sagbado Avoeme, Togo

Standing with
M. Hubert Kponton,
Director of the
National Museum,
in front of Boutique
Togo à Gogo and
wearing one of our
products

Interior of Boutique
Togo à Gogo,
Summer 1968

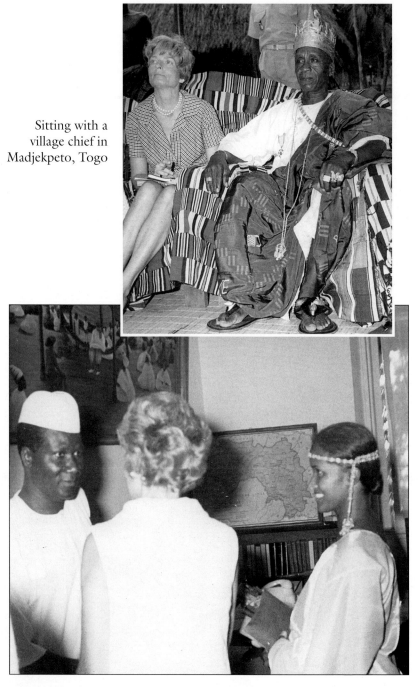

Sitting with a
village chief in
Madjekpeto, Togo

Actress Marpessa Dawn and Guinea's Sékou Touré

The ambassador's residence in Conakry

Our farewell party from Conakry, Guinea; the entertainers pictured here helped themselves to the contents of the linen closet on their way out

Our arrival in Prague, March 1972

The ambassador's residence in Prague, a contrast to our house in Lomé

The staff of the Prague residence, often in need of diplomatic
solutions among themselves

Albert with President Gerald R. Ford, at the signing of the
Helsinki Final Act, Helsinki, 1975

With Ambassador
Daniel Patrick
Moynihan at the
United Nations,
1976

Later that same year with Ambassador William W. Scranton at the
UN General Assembly, 1976

people. All these boats were working together, so something must have been going according to a plan.

The telephone was ringing constantly now, and we conceived the notion that we should try to record the VOR, which raved on, still without giving any concrete information about what was really going on. Among the many accusations trumpeted over and over was a reference to a "cinquieme colonne". I couldn't imagine who in the Republic of Guinea would understand what that meant. Doug Harwood (Administrative Officer) had telephoned asking permission to leave his house to bring a German citizen, a woman, to the German Ambassador's residence next door to us. Her husband had been killed, but she had not yet been informed. The Ambassador wanted her at his house when he told her. Permission was granted. Having performed his mission, Doug arrived at our place paler than any human I had seen. As he stepped over the threshold, a call came from Charles Koivogui, husband of one of our Embassy employees who had been jailed. All I heard Albert say was, "Vous êtes libre? Elle est à Dakar." The caller had been arrested a while back on charges of anti-government activity. No one expected to see him again.

Now we knew what those offshore boats were doing. The dreaded Boiro Prison near our house must have been opened "a la Bastille". These weird happenings made a little bit of sense all of a sudden. We never heard from him again and we never heard whether or not he made it on to one of the boats.

The German ambassador came over to compose a telegram about his dead and wounded. He had been up since very early in the morning, had not shaved or eaten, and looked very gray. I found Pol Gregoire (Belgian chargé) and Ernest Schmidt (Swiss) sitting on the terrace talking to Albert while Lankes (German ambassador) wrote his telegram. Gregoire claimed to have seen white soldiers in uniform when he passed the gendarmerie (but he later retracted this vision). Rumors were flying like confetti. One was that invaders had taken over both military camps. Another, of course, was that the boats had retreated offshore and would land in another place any minute

The servants were terrified so I sent them all home to their families and we ate the very good sandwiches that had been prepared for our aborted motor trip to Mamou. At the time we had expected to be sitting at the waterfall, la Voile de la Mariée near Kindia, we were instead sitting on our own terrace with the same menu but hardly the same spirit. The firing by this time was weirdly absent. No one could figure out exactly what had happened or what would happen next. We all knew that it couldn't be over.

Karim Bangoura, the Minister of Commerce, telephoned to ask Albert to urge Washington to condemn the invasion. The Foreign Minister (his voice extremely weak and wavering) telephoned with the same message. An hour later, in response to messages sent to the Department by Albert, the State Department asked whether the Guineans would like to have the matter presented to the Security Council. He telephoned Bangoura (whose private number we had obtained on one of his previous calls) who consulted Saifoulaye Diallo (Sékou's closest advisor). They agreed that all signals were GO. They had apparently instructed their ambassador at the U.N. to do that, and they much welcomed the support of the U.S. Sékou sent a telegram to U Thant asking for instant airborne troops. The level of hysteria was clearly mounting.

Firing did not start in earnest again until two o'clock or slightly after. Then it was very constant and close. We closed the house as tightly as we could and came upstairs to stay near the radio. Ernie Schmidt of the Swiss Embassy, called to say he had heard that the invaders were attacking the Chinese and Bulgarian Embassies. This, of course, turned out to be another piece of brilliant fiction. What was really going on was the recapture of the gendarmerie camp. The gun battle lasted three hours. During that time the U.N. Representative, who was our other next-door neighbor, jumped or rather climbed the wall. They had no telephone service when they most needed it. The U.S. ambassador did the same thing to deliver messages. I was sorry not to have a photograph of these great scenes.

The shooting slowed down about five. The battle, for the moment, was over. Still, we had not seen one soldier or one bullet. We knew however, that as soon as the sun went down, the firing would begin again. The radio never stopped talking about the ships that had remained in Guinean territorial waters. They were believed to be planning a second invasion that night. Within a few days the common greeting instead of "hello" became "Prête pour la Revolution!" or "Prête!" for short, especially when answering the telephone. That phrase perhaps gave people a feeling of confidence.

I opened a can of corned beef hash that night for supper. It tasted like pure ambrosia. We went to bed very early because the electricity was off and even though the generator was going and we could have had lights, we did not want to attract attention to the house. So at nine-thirty we turned in, exhausted. Firing was going on sporadically then, as gradually the garden filled with troops. We heard footsteps all night long on the gravel below our window. They may have been firing at something, but I rather suspect they were just firing. From midnight on, the machine gun and rifle fire never stopped. Somewhere in the town was an enormous weapon or perhaps only a signal to frighten away the invaders. It made two frightening and ear-shattering blasts at intervals during the night. As far as I know, no one has determined exactly where the mysterious blasts originated, but they were guaranteed to add to the many intrusions into a person's usual sleep pattern.

Monday, November 23, 1970
We got up very early, there being no point in staying in bed. I didn't expect any servants because of the terrible night we had had (and they are fasting now as it is Ramadan), but Diallo was down in the kitchen making breakfast with shooting still going on, although not any more in our own garden. He mumbled something like "gunfire doesn't frighten me" and pulled up his left trouser leg to reveal the most gruesome scarring I have ever seen. "Dien Bien Phu," he added in his usual emotionless style. I was shocked and the shock remained as it sank into my reality that Diallo had been in the French army in what later became known as Viet Nam when the French were trying to do what the Americans also failed to do. I asked "When was that, Diallo?" The only answer I got was "a long time ago." By this time I was wide awake.

Albert decided to try to go to the Embassy, driving himself with flag flying. He informed the other officers by telephone and radio that he would stop at the Norlands' house and lead a convoy. The nurse, who lived near us, turned up in her whites while we were still at the breakfast table.

Everyone was eager to get to work. Chris arrived at the office before the rest of them and called me to say that he had had no difficulty getting there, which was a surprise and a relief.

As these events proceeded, we became more and more involved with daily concerns of the Halco Mining Company, a Canadian firm working the bauxite mine, which was on an island not far away but out of sight. I never went there, so I had only hearsay knowledge of its facilities. I knew that the mixed nationality workers (many Americans among them) lived in trailers, some of them crowded because they had all brought children and pets. The pay was worth it, even though the African workers had a tendency to overlook their garbage cans. There was a meeting house, which provided some recreation, and there was a real house for the manager. A new manager had arrived, a Swede, with his wife and two teenagers, elegant furniture and valuable paintings shortly before the invasion started, so he had not had occasion to build up relationships with any government counterparts. In addition, I would judge his diplomatic skills to be limited.

During the ensuing months, everyone out there was subjected to threats and surprise demands by armed soldiers, which often necessitated the intervention of the Embassy. The vice-consuls were as busy as they would ever be again in their careers.

It's very hard to know what to do with yourself during a war if you are not a soldier. Concentrating on a book, either writing one or reading one, is hard unless you are Ernest Hemingway. So you walk around, you look out the window, and finally you do that superconsoling, never-fail ego massage, you wash your hair. That makes you feel much better and even look a little better. The military contingent numbering approximately fifty soldiers in our garden had nothing to do but look out to sea and lean on the plants. They were rapt when I went out to pick flowers close to the house and sat on the terrace arranging them and pretending that nothing had happened. The Voice of the Revolution continued to exhort the population to take up arms (what arms?) and get ready for an invasion, which was sure to come because of the Fifth Column. The U.N. announced that the Security Council had voted unanimously to send an investigating team.

Members of the government were still hard to find. The streets were empty and offices were empty. There was a lot of communication between the embassy and Washington but locally officials were victims of their own propaganda, at least so far. No one was absolutely sure yet about what had really happened and no one wanted to predict how it would turn out. Albert came home for a late lunch. We drank some vodka with the hope that we could fall asleep afterwards. But there was still too much random firing, and the telephone rang every few minutes, so it was no good. The great blessing bestowed in the late afternoon was that the electricity came on and we could rest with the windows closed.

Our American workers at the mines and at the embassy were more constantly harassed as the paranoia of the Guinean government increased. The morale of the embassy personnel was amazingly strong in spite of many Guinean government restrictions on our movements around the country and even around the city of Conakry. One day our school bus drove our kids to the international school run by wives from our embassy along its usual route which took it under a bridge which had the bodies of three men hanging from it. They were government officials whose names were well known.

The next day at staff meeting Albert told them all that anyone who wished to transfer from the post would be found another job somewhere else. No one left! I thought it a great compliment to the Ambassador. The U.N. Commission came and went without much change in the tenor of our daily lives. Albert testified to exactly what we had seen and reported that a Peace Corps volunteer who was on the beach with a colleague enjoying a bonfire and some beer had been slightly wounded. Later this simple fact was used as evidence locally that the "invasion" had American involvement for sure. The Cubans and African representatives testified in their accustomed animated way to all sorts of apocryphal events, which they claimed to know, either from first-hand knowledge or reliable sources. I learned later from a Polish diplomat at the U.N. who had been a member of that commission that even though members of the panel had requested a tour of the sites mentioned in the testimony, they had been sequestered at the airport and were never shown anything, which was perhaps why the "invasion" received practically no notice in the international press either then or later.

All foreigners were restricted to their residences after 7:30 p.m. by order of the government, which meant that social life came to a virtual halt. The Germans, Swiss, and Belgians had withdrawn their embassies. I went to the Germans' house next door to inventory and oversee the packing of their personal effects and foodstuffs remembering all the time that someone had done the same for me when we left Budapest.

Nonsense from the government cooled down gradually, and threats against our personnel diminished. One time, however, the General Services Officer was picked up by police for a minor infraction of the traffic rules. He was taken to the police station and locked up, even though he had asserted his diplomatic immunity. Albert was so annoyed that he jumped in his official car and went to the station and successfully demanded the young man's immediate release. This encounter knit the staff closer together even than it had been before. Years later when this man was appointed ambassador, he invited me to his swearing-in ceremony at the State Department which I attended with much pride and pleasure.

Our food during this difficult time came from two sources: Oosterman-Peterson, the famous Danish mail order supplier of foodstuffs known to all personnel of embassies, businesses, and other establishments located off the beaten track, and Socomer, a supermarket built by the Yugoslavs which offered a variety of products, food and household goods, but not necessarily inventory a person could count on. Never mind, if you needed coat hangers you should buy a lot at once. The store was attractive and gradually became a sort of social center. I met Stokely Carmichael there one day after the "invasion," wearing army camouflage and carrying a .38 or .45 pistol. When I said "Stokely, why are you all dressed up?" he replied, "They're out to get me. I have to be ready".

I didn't ask who "they" were because I didn't want to give him a chance to say something untrue and negative about the CIA. At this time he was living with Miriam Makeba, who was living with Sékou, or so we thought, a convenient "ménage à trois". Occasionally she would perform at one of the innumerable events we were required to attend. She was indeed so lovely and so talented that her appearance was a godsend. The Chinese had built a white marble edifice known as the Palace of Culture where we were summoned by the Foreign Minister at painfully frequent intervals to watch amateurish artistic events. They regularly started two hours late. Now I look back and fail to understand why we always turned up on time.

The same was true of performances and military exercises in the stadium built by the Russians. The best show I ever saw in that setting was on the occasion of the celebration of the union of Guinea and Ghana, which had been declared by executive fiat between Sékou and Nkrumah, President of Ghana. What I remember most vividly about that particular program was the two presidents, both handsome, dressed in their white robes, sitting on the folded fabric roof top of a convertible white Cadillac riding round and round in the stadium waving while the crowd cheered. Further than that, I remember only that the union lasted a very short time. I guess sharing power was not as much fun as anticipated.

As the social restrictions gradually eased, we began to have parties when visitors from Washington came. The guest list was restricted to members of the government, but as usual when the party lights went on in the garden (strings of multi-colored Christmas tree lights, a tradition everywhere in West Africa) everybody who passed by joined the party. They felt no need to identify themselves or greet the hostess. This would have surprised and perhaps annoyed me more had I not encountered a version of it in Togo. We always had a twenty-four-hour guard at the gate who must have known who would be suitable, a new kind of social secretary. On one of these occasions we were in danger of running out of food, which would have been judged a cardinal sin. The chef, a jolly character trained to a real French cuisine, performed a miracle. He took a frozen barracuda, which Bud had caught months before we were sequestered, out of the freezer and somehow managed to get it on the buffet table beautifully garnished with parsley between its teeth before the guests started to notice that supplies were low. I should have known that people came for conviviality and more, invited or not. I should have known because of a report to me by Fadiala Keita, Guinean Ambassador in Washington when he came to call on us at home in Conakry.

When the beautiful movie star Marpessa Dawn came to visit us just after we arrived in Guinea we had shown her movie "Black Orpheus" (French version) three nights in a row to different audiences. It was a chance to meet many prominent citizens and the guests were delighted to come but we had not served dinner. That, he said, was a faux pas that had reached him all the way across the sea. I stopped trying to do things in any kind of "original" way. Popcorn and soft drinks, what's that? Consequently I never forgot, hospitality without a meal is perceived as no hospitality, at least in the home of the American Ambassador.

The assignment to Guinea was tough, but it ended better than could have been anticipated, I judge now looking back. When our impending departure was announced, Sékou invited Albert and me to lunch/dinner. There was only one other guest, Saifoulaye Diallo, Foreign Minister. The table might have been called a refectory table, long and narrow. I sat opposite Sékou and must have had both forearms on the table because toward the end of the meal, he took both of my wrists in one of his hands, the better to get my attention, while he explained once again that Africa would "make it" someday and I should tell everyone I know. At that moment I believed. He was a powerful, sexy person.

I hired a Guinean band and a dance group of women to perform at our farewell party which was literally a howling success. I wore one of my African dresses and did a dance with the group, not well of course because no one else can move the way they do, but well enough so my audience knew what I was trying to do, and they loved it. Meanwhile the extra dancers were investigating the contents of the cupboards in their dressing room, which contained table and bed linen. A few days later when we were packing up, the disappearance of the entire contents of that closet was reported to me, which set me to wondering how Santa Claus from the Christmas cloth looked on a nice plump derriere as it waddled down the main street or maybe into one of those solemn meetings of organized women in the name of one of Conakry's neighborhood organizations. "Prête pour la revolution!"

So ended one of the most bizarre chapters of my Foreign Service life. I had used all my skills. I had smiled when I felt like crying and had never permitted myself to write my mother the whole truth. I understood finally why the wretched of the earth continue to be wretched, a mystery to most people. So that was a bonus. Hubris is a very destructive thing and so is self-pity, its coefficient in the equation. One or the other will explain any circumstance. If preached long enough by a convincing leader, the people will believe anything and accept willingly the official explanations of the crises as they come along. The result is that progress is very slow and sometimes force is needed to quell the influence of a self-declared hero. In several cases a takeover is made simple by the murder of the strong, educated leader by a power-seeking pretender. Typical was the case in Togo where the first President of the fledgling republic, Sylvanus Olympio, said to have been the African representative of Lever Bros., a large British manufacturing company, was fatally shot as he got out of his car to go into his residence (which happened to be located next door to the American Embassy). During the next fifteen years the graft, favoritism, and abuses of human rights gradually increased to depressing proportions while the wretched population cowered. This trend has not abated. One can only weep for them and wait.

CHAPTER THIRTEEN

Tricks and Treats

A WELCOME CHANGE WAS IN STORE. We were told that the next stop was a return to tricky old Prague where we felt we would be on familiar ground. We knew almost every inch of our residence, the Pejcek Palace as it was known after the family who built it in 1928. Mythology told us that the rich coal baron who caused it to be constructed took his whole family west in a railroad car as soon as the hot breath of Hitler was felt in the region. His cousin, not to be outdone, built a palace very similar, which ended up in the hands of the Russians, to this day a very interesting fact to tourists. We were always told that the United States Treasury used Czech crowns accumulated from the sale of surplus military supplies left behind by General Eisenhower to buy the palace. Eisenhower liberated Czechoslovakia from its western border as far as Pilsen, while the Russians approached from the East as part of the plan supposedly hatched by Stalin *et al.* at the famous Yalta Conference. It is impossible to imagine how different contemporary European history would be if the Americans, always true to their word in those days, had instead just kept on going all the way at least to Prague. The whole country would have landed in the Western camp where culturally and psychologically it had always belonged.

Driving in through the gorgeous, pretentious Pejcek palace gateway was, for me, a blood-pressure raiser. When we entered the foyer we found the staff lined up in rank order starting with the chef, the same one who had held that important post when we lived in Prague twenty years earlier. We greeted each other with a real embrace, and he introduced the others, the kitchen maid, the butler, two upstairs maids and the laundress who, together with the woman I later engaged as a sort of "chef de cabinet" and secretary, were in constant battle formation. The Czechs, more than other Eastern Europeans I had known, were always argumentative, defensive, and generally hard to deal with. Was it because Jan Huss wrecked the influence of the Catholic Church and left nothing very solid behind? Or was it possibly because they were educated to be defensive, not having fought since the Battle of the White Mountain (1780) in which they were defeated by the Austrians? Time after time they ran up the white flag while the Poles would attack tanks with primitive weapons if they perceived their freedom threatened. The excuse always was that they were avoiding destruction of their beautiful city.

A look at world-famous Czech literature, mostly dark tales, reveals something perhaps. Franz Kafka? Josef Capek? Milan Kundera? The so-called "Prague uprising of 1968" when followers of Alexander Dubček demanded more freedom from the Soviet Union seemed to have been forgotten. The whole country was depressed again. They had thought for a few precious days that they had succeeded in ridding themselves of dreaded communism, so when the Russian tanks rolled in and serious fighting began, the damage inflicted was more psychological than anything else.

Albert and I had a running start not only because we were familiar with the setting but also because of a remarkable art collection lent by Mr. and Mrs. Stanley Woodward, private collectors, and residents of Washington, D.C., who livened many an embassy by their extraordinary generosity in lending large consignments of their very rich personal collection. He had been a Foreign Service Officer and later an Ambassador to Canada so he and his wife Shirley knew how undistinguished some embassies are. That could not be said of the "Pejcek Palace" but the interest and quality the collection gave to that remarkable house is hard to describe. It became an even more precious jewel.

I think it was the Department of State that funded publication of a first-class catalogue in a large quantity so that we really had enough to distribute generously. I went to great pains gradually to call on every known artist in his studio and found every one eager to receive me. Usually we spoke French but my Czech lessons were gradually beginning to show results. In other words I was beginning to differentiate it from Polish. Many of the words are the same, but the sound of the languages is quite different, every Czech word being accented on the first syllable which makes it sound harsh, whereas Polish accents every word on the penultimate syllable making it less staccato and softer.

Using my newfound credentials as an art afficionado because of the Woodward's collection, I asked the Director of the National Museum whom I had come to know quite well where I could go to learn how to restore oil paintings, a skill I had always found interesting and I realized that possibly never again in my life might I find the leisure to pursue the idea. He immediately offered to arrange for me to go the restoration department of his museum to learn how it was done in Prague, saying that if I wished to pursue it further he would find me a teacher. I was, of course, delighted and grateful for this effort on his part which extended to introducing me to the Head of the Department, a charming but at the same time matter-of-fact woman who had obviously prepared for a new worker because there was an easel with a damaged portrait of Simon Bolívar sitting on it where the director invited me to sit down and start gingerly removing the last coat of shellac with a turpentine sponge. I was quite nervous, afraid I would ruin beyond repair a painting of some value. But when she showed me the painting I was to work on under an X-ray I saw that the canvas had several layers of paintings on it, none worth saving. The charming woman returned several times to see if I was happy at my work and I told her I was.

This went on for several weeks, once a week. I began to notice that each time I went, the charming woman was a touch less charming. Maybe the novelty had worn off. Finally when I went and found my easel set up in the bathroom, I realized that in fact I was not welcome any more or maybe I never had been. What were the state secrets that I was not supposed to see? Obviously the Director of the museum had made a mistake and was told to get out of it somehow. I can't say I was really surprised and I did learn enough to refinish an old portrait of George Washington that hung in our house in Connecticut. It is still there reminding me of the charming woman and her boss, the Director.

We had a great many visitors, official visitors, in those days because people all over the West were holding their collective breath to welcome in the demolition of the Iron Curtain, which you could feel was coming soon. Prague, with its democratic leanings and history of Tomas Mazaryk, the first President of Czechoslovakia and a close friend of President Woodrow Wilson, and his son Jan Mazaryk, who later became Foreign Minister, made a fine backdrop for leadership emanating from that quarter.

Because of the many visitors whom I shepherded in the city, I eventually came to know it quite well. One of my favorite places to take people was the old synagogue, said to have been built in the year 900 A.D. The building tells many stories. One is that these days there were not enough men (thirteen at minimum are needed) in the orthodox community to hold services. So the place was always open for tourists and there were always enough official guides to show people around. I became well enough versed in the lore of that holy place and its fascinating cemetery to show people around without a hired guide. The tombstones were piled indiscriminately, lapping over each other at odd angles. I was told that the Nazis, as they had pogroms in the villages, brought the stones to Prague and dumped them there in the cemetery beside the old synagogue.

In the middle of the tombstones is the grave of the famous Rabbi Lev. It has a three-foot-high surround which makes it look almost like a bed with taller peaked pieces of stone at each end. A cover protects the contents of the bed but not quite. It is through the gap that people send their written messages to the rabbi, mostly wish lists. This famous and much-revered rabbi is said to have created out of mud a creature called the Golem, a monster intended to help the people with their work in mysterious ways at night. According to the mythology, the Golem performed his tasks over an extended period of time, but finally he turned into a monster and became destructive. No one knows where he is now, but possibly he will turn up again in some new mysterious way. The people did not seem to blame Rabbi Lev for letting this genie out of the bottle. Golem fit in with their generally dark and uncontrollable view of life. The lesser stones had names incised on them in Hebrew and usually a charming figure—a fish (Fischer), a deer (Hirsch), scissors (Schneider), a tree (Baum)—so the identities of the people whose stones lie there were not completely lost. It was Maria Theresa who forced the Jews, for tax purposes, to submit their real names. Many of these names they have kept down the generations to the present time.

One evening as I was dressing for a formal dinner at our house, the telephone in my bedroom rang. It was Pan Lečko (the chef) calling from the kitchen. He said, "Madam, there has been an accident in the house." His French was not always correct, but always comprehensible. Lord, I thought, he's done it again! I was thinking of the time he sliced his own nose with the back of a butcher knife when he was so angry with the kitchen maid that he chopped too vigorously for his own good.

But that wasn't it this time. He told me there was a Russian citizen in the house waiting to speak to me in one of the rooms on the ground floor, the room known as the "herren salon". He only wanted to speak to me, no one else, and right away. I really could not go there at that moment because I had to greet our guests. So I telephoned Bud's Deputy Chief of Mission whose house was conveniently located just across the garden. He was a fluent Russian speaker, a gentle, intelligent person. Afterwards he told me this fantastic explanation: the man said he was a tourist who learned on the bus he rode that afternoon the location of the American ambassador's residence where he had decided to go to seek political asylum. Somehow Art was able to persuade him that we had no power to grant political asylum at the house or anywhere else so he had better leave. The man finally accepted this advice without disturbing Bud and me as we entertained our guests in a nearby room before going in to dinner. By the time we had to walk through the room where he had been talking to Art, they were both gone. Obviously the bad guys just wanted to know how I would react and the kitchen staff must have been told to allow the man to enter.

As had been my previous experience in Prague, I had constant trouble with the servants. I had hired as my secretary the woman who was teaching me Czech. She was a cultivated person and could be relied on to handle the invitations both outgoing and incoming reliably. Her English was good so she could deal with people staying in the house, even when I was not at home. In short, she was invaluable to me. She had, however, one unforgivable flaw. She thought she was better than the other servants in the house because she was from a family higher on the social scale and better educated and, especially in that kind of socialist world, they resented her instead of laughing at her. They did everything they could think of to undermine her authority, including stealing objects of value from my personal possessions and claiming no knowledge of them. As she was supposed to be the go-between for me so I would be spared listening to every bleat, there were plenty of occasions to make her look foolish. In retrospect, I should have fired her, but the difficulty of finding a suitable replacement always stopped me. Whenever she sensed that I was getting fed up, she would tell me a wild tale about what she had to sacrifice in order to work at the American embassy. She asked me one afternoon, for instance, if I knew how difficult it was for her son because of his mother's employment. He was in the army and, she said, was demoted the previous day because of her job. I said I thought that was unfair but I took it with a grain of salt. Exaggeration was her normal mode.

CHAPTER FOURTEEN

Real Diplomacy

SEEMINGLY OUT OF THE BLUE came an order to Albert to go to Geneva to head the American Delegation to the CSCE (Conference on Security and Cooperation in Europe) which had been meeting for a couple of years before we got there. It turned out to be the instrument that ultimately did bring down the Berlin Wall and subsequently end the Cold War. If that seems like an exaggeration, it must be agreed at least that it gave courage and impetus to freedom movements all across Europe, because finally they had a document defining freedom of travel, freedom of the press and speech, the whole list of what had always been referred to as "fundamental freedoms". One of its most promising features was that it provided for a follow-up meeting in two years to check on adherence to the agreement.

This surprising document was taken literally by many thinkers and politicians in Eastern Europe, providing a constant river of hope which was faithfully reported on in all the Western European press, information bound to seep over all the borders. Albert was to maintain his embassy in Prague simultaneously so we started in on another balancing act during which we would use every trick we had ever learned in the Foreign Service. I decided to drive my little Ford sports car so I could be independent and go back and forth whenever I felt it necessary. In order to do this I had to overnight in Munich, which I always enjoyed, the museums having been restored along with the rest of West Germany. We needed only a few possessions in Geneva because our U.N. Mission there had rented a charming furnished apartment and provided a driver, so we really had no settling-in to do. It was glorious. I hadn't lived that way for so long; or maybe I never had. There was a cleaning service once a week so I had no need even to change the sheets. I learned cooking all over again and appreciated the adventure of shopping in the Swiss grocery stores, a real pleasure. I say the apartment was charming, but it was more than that. It was a miracle of design. No greater contrast could be imagined to our huge baroque palace in Prague. It consisted of two rooms, a mini kitchen and bath. The two rooms were unique in my experience, an elegantly furnished living room and a dining room, which turned into a bedroom once the table was folded up and the two Murphy beds were lowered. The décor was a sort of baroque attempt, the colors turquoise and cream reminiscent of a room of the palace at Schoenbruhn, the ultimate in show-off. Nevertheless, when the curtains were closed in the evening it became a very cozy place.

My youngest brother was already a delegate to the Conference before we arrived. He had been in the legal office of the Department of State in Washington and had been assigned as legal counsel to the delegation, which, of course, added much to my personal pleasure, although it didn't last long. How many raclette dinners did we enjoy together? At the same time there was a close watch by the legal section of the delegation on the proposals the delegation was planning. This was to prevent any agreements that could run contra to other commitments the U.S. might have made or contra to provisions in the U.S. Constitution.

As time went on participants became more and more enthusiastic as they sensed that a significant achievement was in sight. I have wondered often how the East European countries managed to allow it to happen because in the long run the CSCE changed profoundly the history of all of Europe and in just the way the West wanted. Governments of the Eastern bloc agreed to freedom of travel, freedom of the press free elections, free assembly, and much more that the East had been denied ever since communism was introduced after World War II.

Meanwhile when I felt I needed to return to check on the general state of affairs in Prague, I would drive back to spend a few days. One time when Philip Roth was visiting with one of his girlfriends, it happened to be a period of stalemate between the United States and the Czechs in the negotiations relating to restitution of gold commandeered by the Nazis during the war and later held in safekeeping by the United States. Our Congress was also making it difficult to come to an agreement, so negotiations were protracted.

Because the bilateral relations between our two countries were not going well, the Czech authors and other literary figures who were invited to a luncheon in Roth's honor declined the invitation, and we ended up with a collection of students, which was all right with me. The secretary ordered flowers from Holland as instructed and laid the table with Meissen china, which belonged to the house.

Finally Philip Roth arrived, late. We had a drink and then sat down at our place cards. Eventually he turned to me and asked, "And what do you do?"

I was stunned. I took a few seconds to reply and then I said one word, "Nothing".

He turned away and had no more to say. He was in Prague to spend some Czech crowns accumulated in his bank account there. Why was I giving a luncheon for him? It made me curse privately. The Foreign Service was terrible sometimes.

Back in Geneva things were going well. The utmost in diplomatic skill was required, but eventually (August 1975) the remarkable document was ready for signing and the delegates went to Helsinki for the signing ceremony as had been agreed on years before. There they were joined by their chiefs of state and a solemn ceremony was held in which thirty-five of them signed a document signifying a turning point in the history of Europe. The most miraculous part about it for me was seeing Gerald Ford and Albert Sherer working together just as Jerry had predicted almost thirty years before. Unfortunately I witnessed it only on the television because by the time August came around I was too lonesome for my children to stay away, so I went to the family place in Michigan where we were all together, my whole family. Albert followed quickly.

CHAPTER FIFTEEN

What It Really Takes

LONG BEFORE WE LEFT GENEVA, it was settled that we would go next to the United Nations. We knew a little bit about that because in 1953 when the U.N. was still a novelty and the wonderful Dag Hammerskjold was the Secretary General, the State Department sent Albert and a number of other young Foreign Service Officers up to New York to help out during the General Assembly. Their job was to keep their ears to the ground and try to determine how the delegates intended to vote. Afterwards he always referred to this group as the "bathroom brigade". Apparently valuable information could be picked up in that location if a person knew what questions to ask and to whom. At that time there were only about 60 members. Now there are 192, which will continue to change as countries reconfigure themselves.

The United States always maintains four or more ambassadors there who serve different functions but the one the public is most likely to be aware of is the boss, called the "Permanent Representative", although he is often a political appointee and therefore the least permanent of them all. The Perm Rep has a deputy who is usually a career diplomat.

Otherwise the Mission is divided into sections rather like an embassy with a special ambassador responsible for guest-country issues. The foreign representatives need a lot of coddling and support. I suspect that many of them leave the United States after years and still fail to realize that their diplomatic license plates do not give them *carte blanche* to park anywhere they like. Albert was Deputy Ambassador to the Security Council, which meant that whenever the two ambassadors who outranked him did not choose to sit in the chair marked UNITED STATES OF AMERICA, it was his job. However, since that was a favorite place to be, he had plenty of time to devote to the behind-the-scenes challenging work which is always going on at the U.N. and which takes real diplomatic skills which career men and women have supposedly acquired by the time they reach the ambassadorial level. So Albert's work was mostly on other questions.

A Soviet diplomat working in the U.N. Secretariat, for instance, decided to defect. At that time, engineering it so that his bosses were unaware of what was happening was tricky. What the U.S. always tries to do in such a case is to "defect the candidate in place" which means to convince the person that he or she will be well enough protected so that he can safely continue working while informing his minders of everything he does and with whom. Daniel Patrick Moynihan, an excitable Irishman, was the Perm Rep at that time who found this development exhilarating, so much so that part of the game became the difficulty of keeping it secret.

Working for Pat and Liz Moynihan was a real treat, as they were both so intelligent, both so engaged. As I look back on my life, I have to admit to myself that the things I said "no" to would have been the most amusing and

instructive. Pat asked me if I would like a job as his simultaneous translator in French, and I said "no thank you"
when I should have said *yes*. I can only figure now that it
was because I was having too much fun in New York and
more fun working with a good architect on remodeling our
Connecticut house to want to be tied down to someone
else's schedule as I had been for so many years. I will always
regret it.

When Pat became a Senator from New York, Gerald
Ford nominated William Scranton, a former governor of
Pennsylvania and an old Yale friend of Albert's. The
appointment was not yet announced but Bill and his wife,
Mary, on separate telephones called to find out whether
his friend thought he would do well in the job and to ask
general questions about conditions and content of the
work. The truth is, I can't imagine a personality better
suited to it. Bill had no pretenses. He was universally
respected, trusted, and admired. He knew what he didn't
know. The heavy-duty social life was not a pleasure, but
he was already a professional politician so he understood
how to play the game and what was its purpose. Bill asked
Bud to find him a good secretary right away. Bud sacri-
ficed his own marvel woman, a super-efficient person, an
old-timer in the Foreign Service, whom he had known
since our days in Togo. No encomiums are excessive for
the way she played her role as right hand to the chief. I
think very soon he really enjoyed his job.

We were having a splendid time getting pretty much
what we wanted at the U.N. until President Carter was
elected. Someone must have told him that it was custom-
ary for every new president to appoint his own representatives to the U.N. because he did that right away; we left and

went back to our summer place to see what would happen next. The new President appointed Andrew Young, a well-known civil rights worker at the time. I was present when they gave their first addresses and was aware of the audible shock when each one placed an ankle on the opposite knee the way Americans like to do.

In Europe showing the bottom of a shoe is considered rude. Remember when Adlai Stevenson did it? The sole had a hole in it, and the press thought it was hilarious. As I recall, he was not addressing the General Assembly at the time. Ambassador Young lasted only a short time because the story told was that he went off to Cuba to see whether he could settle things in a hurry with Castro. I guess the Secretary of State didn't like that, because Andrew Young went back to civilian life promptly and his deputy, a black career Foreign Service Officer, took over. It was always my impression that he was exceptionally well regarded.

Albert was asked then to head up the U.S. Delegation to the follow-up meeting of the 35 nations who had signed the Helsinki Final Act, scheduled to take place in Belgrade in the fall. Historically it is an exhilarating time. The Wall was not down yet but one felt it in the air. There were rumblings.

We were looking forward to a very interesting task ahead as we rested up and prepared at our country place in Michigan. We were lying on our bed with books when the telephone rang and it is one of the new people at State announcing to Albert that President Carter has appointed Arthur Goldberg, former Supreme Court Justice, to head the delegation to Belgrade, but they hope Albert will agree to go as Goldberg's deputy. Of course he innocently agreed.

The Goldbergs had invited us for cocktails at their apartment with several of the sitting Justices, but that was the only time I saw them until Belgrade, when we were told that the little house reserved for us on embassy property had been reassigned to the Goldbergs who, regarding themselves as particularly vulnerable, had asked that Marine guards be stationed at all times.

We had a very cozy little house also on the campus of the embassy, but we required no guards.

In the end, the Belgrade meeting turned out to be a disaster. The Finnish Ambassador's wife said to me *sotto voce* "Everyone is so sad." I was sorely aware of the sadness because the outcome had been largely our (the United States') fault. It was a new experience for most of the Foreign Service officers there who were accustomed to being able to achieve their goals by means of careful and measured diplomacy, which they knew so well how to achieve. Unfortunately, Goldberg was grandstanding all the time, insisting on being addressed as "Justice" and inviting all his friends including Pearl Bailey, a charming woman, and a large collection of personal acquaintances to join the delegation as though it were the U.N. during the General Assembly. Finally the U.S. accounted for 141 delegates while the French had ten and others their accustomed modest numbers of professional diplomats.

Everyone had had such high hopes for this meeting because the first one had been so successful. At the conclusion, the U.S. Ambassador to Yugoslavia, Lawrence Eagleburger at the time, gave a dinner at his residence honoring Justice Goldberg. Attending the dinner was Governor Nelson Rockefeller and his wife who were visiting the country on a private trip. During the pre-prandial chitchat, the Governor came to me and said, "Please tell the Justice that I hold no personal animosity toward him because of the election." Apparently the Justice had been avoiding him, and that was not Rockefeller's style. I never delivered that message.

When Albert died several years later, I received a heart-warming note from the Justice written in longhand and expressing a kind of respect and sensitivity that I had never suspected he possessed. I don't think that the sympathy expressed showed that political appointees, no matter how intelligent, understand what motivates those who are professional diplomats working not only with their brains but with their hearts and a lifetime of carefully honed skills. George Kennan, the scion of the professional Foreign Service in our time had this to say about it in a speech to the Foreign Service Association.

"This is the classic function of diplomacy: to effect the communication between one's own government and other governments or individuals abroad, and to do this with maximum accuracy, imagination, tact, and good sense.... What is important in the relations between governments is not just the "what" but rather the "how", the approach, the posture, the style, the manner of action. The most brilliant undertaking can be turned into a failure if it is clumsily and tactlessly executed; there are, on the other hand, few blunders which cannot be survived, if not redeemed, when matters are conducted with grace and with feeling...."

To some extent, I fear, the professional diplomatist will always remain in his own country, and particularly in this one, a person apart, the bearer of a view of the outside world, which his fellow citizens cannot entirely fol-

low, and a view of his own country which, although it does not cause him to love it the less, causes him to see it in other ways than his neighbors can be expected to see it... For these reasons, diplomacy is always going to consist to some extent of serving people who do not know that they are being served, who do not know that they need to be served, who misunderstand and occasionally, abuse the very effort to serve...it takes a special love of country to pursue, with love, and faith, and cheerfulness, work for which no parades will ever march, no crowds will cheer, no bands will play....

Every word of this speech is as true today as it was when Ambassador Kennan delivered it to young FSO's in 1961. Even the great United States cannot afford to have a shameful number of unkept promises on record. We are no longer trusted the way we would like to be, a situation which no one desires or intended. We are baffled. We are asking, "How did this calamitous situation come about and so suddenly?" The "greats" in our population are rare specimens in Washington now. We long for a party that can lead from strength, not push. It may be inspired from the bottom, from the young, from another "greatest generation" that is waiting in the wings to be put to work. These lions are restlessly growling at the gates telling us that it is their turn.

Afterword

T HIS LITTLE VOLUME COULD NOT have been put together without the skill of my daughter Susan Sherer Osnos. She guided me with professional know-how and diligence. I owe an equal debt to her husband Peter Osnos who gave my feeble start an energetic shove by reading the half-finished manuscript and declaring that it had sufficient merit to finish.

He also introduced me to Della Mancuso, who managed the production of this book, and designer Mary Kornblum. They were generous with their time, and full of excellent suggestions which prevented any number of faux pas. I would also like to thank my friend Lucy Stille for reading the manuscript as I approached the end of this project.

Finally, I will always be grateful to the many characters in this book who contributed to these experiences.